PHILOSOPHY
BITES

DAVID EDMONDS &
NIGEL WARBURTON

OXFORD
UNIVERSITY PRESS

OXFORD
UNIVERSITY PRESS

Great Clarendon Street, Oxford OX2 6DP

Oxford University Press is a department of the University of Oxford.
It furthers the University's objective of excellence in research, scholarship,
and education by publishing worldwide in

Oxford New York

Auckland Cape Town Dar es Salaam Hong Kong Karachi
Kuala Lumpur Madrid Melbourne Mexico City Nairobi
New Delhi Shanghai Taipei Toronto

With offices in

Argentina Austria Brazil Chile Czech Republic France Greece
Guatemala Hungary Italy Japan Poland Portugal Singapore
South Korea Switzerland Thailand Turkey Ukraine Vietnam

Oxford is a registered trade mark of Oxford University Press
in the UK and in certain other countries

Published in the United States
by Oxford University Press Inc., New York

British Library Cataloguing in Publication Data

Data available

Library of Congress Cataloging in Publication Data

Data available

Typeset by SPI Publisher Services, Pondicherry, India
Printed in Great Britain
on acid-free paper by
Clays Ltd., St Ives plc

ISBN 978–0–19–957632–6

1 3 5 7 9 10 8 6 4 2

To Liz, and to Anna

PREFACE

This book began as a series of podcast audio interviews. We have selected—with some difficulty—twenty-five of these to include here from a total of well over a hundred. In the first three years of the podcast we've had over 7 million downloads, fan-mail from all over the world, and many requests for transcripts—hence the book.

One distinguished philosopher whom we asked for an interview turned us down because he disapproved of the Internet. But happily he proved a rare exception. For the most part those we've approached have been remarkably cooperative and supportive. For us, one of the principal benefits of running *Philosophy Bites* has been our free weekly seminar. So our first debt is to our interviewees, and not just those who feature in this book, but all the philosophers who've succumbed to our gentle interrogations. It has been a privilege for us to meet so many interesting and significant thinkers.

Our second debt is to our listeners. We've had an amazing amount of feedback—emails of support every day, often with recommendations for whom we should interview next. This has been very gratifying.

For this volume, the interviews with Peter Singer and with Michael Sandel were originally recorded for the Open University's podcast series *Ethics Bites* (www.open2.net/ethicsbites) and we are grateful for permission to reproduce them here.

Several of the interviews were recorded in the Institute of Philosophy, London, and we are very grateful for their collaboration with that.

Thanks to Hannah Edmonds, whose former life as a proofreader/editor has been exploited once again. And thanks too to our agents Veronique Baxter and Caroline Dawnay.

David Edmonds and Nigel Warburton
www.philosophybites.com

CONTENTS

ix

CONTENTS

INTRODUCTION

Philosophy began as dialogue. Socrates famously would write nothing down. He just quizzed his contemporaries in the marketplace on the topics they felt most certain about. Without exception he showed that their certainty was misplaced. Fortunately Plato reconstructed his conversations.

Of course, the fact that philosophy had its roots in dialogue doesn't mean that it should always be interactive in that way. Most of the great philosophers in history have presented their ideas to the world in the form of books, long monologues typically. This is still true today. What a dialogue can offer, though, is explanation. The questioner can stop the flow and seek clarification, or throw in an apparent counter-example so as better to understand what the other person means. The spirit of philosophy is at its most apparent in conversation—the probing, the teasing out of opinions, the search for reasons and justifications.

Professional philosophers spend a great deal of their time talking to each other, and to their students. But the wider public doesn't have access to these discussions. Part of our mission is to show what an exciting subject philosophy can be, to convey the enthusiasm for ideas that can be hard to communicate in a book-length tract.

Each interview focuses on a single topic and is deliberately short and to the point—bite-sized. Philosophy need not be obscure, and it shouldn't be inaccessible. Nor need the communication of its ideas be 'Philosophy Lite'. Often the most brilliant philosophers are also those most willing and able to convey their thoughts to an intelligent non-specialist audience.

One of the more gratifying aspects of this project has been the encouragement and support we have received, with numerous listeners telling us how important thinking about philosophical issues is for them. Many people prefer reading to listening. Or if they have listened to something, they like to be able to go back to it in written form and locate key ideas. Many people like a book on their shelf too, or an e-book on their e-book reader. But a verbatim transcript of a spoken interview won't necessarily preserve the meaning. Consequently, we have asked contributors to revise their interviews slightly so that they can stand alone on the page. We have also given some indications of further reading on each topic.

Philosophy is an unusual subject in that its practitioners don't agree what it's about. The first section of the book—'What is Philosophy?'—puzzled and amused us. When we started asking interviewees for a definition of their discipline, no two answers came back the same. One interviewee just laughed. Although there are common themes, some of the answers are radically different. We felt that this overlapping diversity of opinion was worth preserving and reproduce it here.

The *Philosophy Bites* podcasts are ongoing. For this book we have selected interviews on particular topics in philosophy. For a later one we will focus on interviews about great philosophers. All our podcast interviews are available free from www.philosophybites. com, where there is also a link to an email address.

WHAT IS PHILOSOPHY?

We asked a range of our interviewees for our *Philosophy Bites* podcast the simple question 'What is Philosophy?' They had no warning of the question. Their answers surprised us. The combination of perspectives was illuminating. Here they are in alphabetical order.

Marilyn Adams: *Philosophy is thinking really hard about the most important questions and trying to bring analytic clarity both to the questions and the answers.*

Robert Adams: *Philosophy is what philosophers do. That's important because I don't want to be narrow as to what constitutes philosophy. There are certain ways of doing philosophy that are sufficiently different from the way that I and a majority of English-speaking philosophers do it, that I might hesitate to say they and we are practising the same discipline. But I think it would be unduly imperialistic to say what they're doing is not philosophy.*

Peter Adamson: *Wow. I guess I think philosophy is the study of the costs and benefits that accrue when you take up a certain position. For example, if you're arguing about free will and you're trying to decide whether to be a compatibilist or incompatibilist—is free will compatible with causal determinism?—what you're discovering is what problems and what benefits you get from saying that it is compatible, and what problems and benefits you get from saying it's incompatible.*

John Armstrong: *Philosophy is the successful love of thinking.*

Catalin Avramescu: *You've hit me with this question. It's a little bit like what Augustine famously said about the concept of time. When nobody asks me about it, I know. But whenever somebody asks me about what the concept of time is, I realize I don't know.*

Simon Blackburn: *Well, it's a process of reflection on the deepest concepts, that is structures of thought, that make up the way in which we think about the world. So it's concepts like reason, causation, matter, space, time, mind, consciousness, free will, all those big abstract words and they make up topics, and people have been thinking about them for two and a half thousand years and I expect they'll think about them for another two and half thousand years if there are any of us left.*

Richard Bradley: *Philosophy is 99 per cent about critical reflection on anything you care to be interested in.*

Wendy Brown: *Philosophy asks about life's meanings. Philosophy asks about who we are, what we might be, how we conceive ourselves, and how we can even think these questions.*

Allen Buchanan: *I don't think it's any one thing, but I think generally it involves being critical and reflective about things that most people take for granted.*

John Campbell: *I don't think there is a general answer to that question. The thing that interests me most is what science is telling us about our common-sense picture of the world. What I'm uneasy about is a doublethink where on the one hand we just operate uncritically with our common-sense picture of the world, and then we shift into scientific mode. I think science really destabilizes our common-sense picture of the* *world. Understanding just where common sense has to give in the face of the science, where common sense is consistent with science, and where we have some real work to do to understand how they can both be correct—that is really what drives me.*

Clare Carlisle: *Most simply put it's about making sense of all this ... We find ourselves in a world that we haven't chosen. There are all sorts of possible ways of interpreting it and finding meaning in the world and in the lives that we live. So philosophy is about making sense of that situation that we find ourselves in.*

Tony Coady: *Oh, well I'm an analytic philosopher, so I'm committed to the view that philosophy involves a lot of analytic work: a lot of analysis of concepts. But I think some people think philosophy only involves analysing concepts and getting clear about things. They also think you should have arguments for everything—it's a very argumentative profession. These are all features of philosophy. But philosophy should also be aiming to do rather more synthetic large-scale sorts of things. Philosophy should be concerned with issues to do with the meaning of life, ethical and political issues, and should be scrutinizing the basic assumptions of our society. Philosophy has always been something of a science of presuppositions; but it shouldn't just expose them and say 'there they are'. It should say something further about them that can help people. As I get older and older I'm more and more concerned that there should be more imagination in philosophy than there is. At one stage it was all very clever, but rather dry. Although I would never want to get quite as imaginative as the various post-structuralist philosophers who put such a premium on imagination that the analysis and argument drop out, I still think that there's something in offering a big picture about our circumstances, and I think that that's something that should be encouraged in philosophy.*

Tim Crane: *To quote Wilfrid Sellars, philosophy is the attempt to understand how things in the most general sense of that word hang together in the most general sense of those words.*

Roger Crisp: *I think it's something you have to do to understand its essence.*

Don Cupitt: *Philosophy is critical thinking: trying to become aware of how one's own thinking works, of all the things one takes for granted, of the way in which one's own thinking shapes the things one's thinking about.*

Donna Dickenson: *Philosophy is what I was told as an undergraduate women couldn't do—by an eminent philosopher who had best remain nameless. But for me it's the gadfly image, the Socratic gadfly: refusing to accept any platitudes or accepted wisdom without examining it.*

John Dunn: *I think it used to be an enquiry into what's true and how people should live; it's distantly related to that still, but I'd say the distance is growing rather than narrowing.*

Luciano Floridi: *Philosophy is conceptual engineering. That means dealing with questions that are open to informed reasonable disagreement by providing new concepts that can be superseded in the future if more economic solutions can be found—but it's a matter of rational agreement.*

Sebastian Gardner: *Philosophy is the attempt to unify theoretical and practical reason.*

Raymond Geuss: *I'm afraid I have a very unhelpful answer to that, because it's only a negative answer. It's the answer that Friedrich Schlegel gave in his Athenaeum Fragments: philosophy is a way of trying to be a systematic spirit without having a system.*

A. C. Grayling: *Philosophy is enquiry into all those things which we don't yet properly and fully understand. When we do get some grip on a problem or a set of problems we can hive that off into a special science or a social science – although those natural and social sciences tend to end up back as* philosophical *problems too—being those problems half obscure, half unformed, where the questions are themselves doubtful, where we're peering out into the dark and don't yet have a good sense of what we're doing. And that's what philosophy is, it's enquiry into the mainly unknown.*

Thomas Hurka: *Philosophy is abstract thought guided by principles of logic and ideals of precision in thought and argumentation about the most general issues concerning human beings and the world and our place in the world.*

Terence Irwin: *Some people have said, and I agree with them, that it's the argument from things that seem perfectly obvious to a conclusion that's extremely surprising. Other people have said that it's a way of trying to get clear about the basic presuppositions of claims we tend to take for granted. Both of these are reasonably good ideas about what philosophy tries to do.*

Chris Janaway: *Um . . . ah . . . that's a very good question. I'm reacting in the sort of way that you would expect philosophers to react; they very often don't give an answer, and people find that suspicious. I suppose philosophy is the attempt to ask questions which seem not to go away—questions which are always going to be there.*

Anthony Kenny: *Philosophy is thinking as clearly as possible about the most fundamental concepts that reach through all the disciplines.*

Chandran Kukathas: *My understanding of philosophy probably owes more to Michael Oakeshott than anybody else. Philosophy is an attempt to think systematically about the presuppositions of a given topic; to try to understand that topic in terms of concepts that give you a complete account of something. So, for example, to the extent that philosophy discusses ethics, it tries to give you an account of what is the nature of morality. Or to the extent that philosophy discusses politics, it tries to give you an account of what politics is in terms of concepts that make sense of this phenomenon.*

Will Kymlicka: *Well I'm in a philosophy department but I'm always wondering what exactly I have in common with many of my colleagues, because, to be frank, I don't necessarily understand the work they do in the philosophy of language or metaphysics. There's a certain element of contingency about what remains in a philosophy department. Philosophy used to encompass economics and so on; and bits and pieces have separated themselves out and become self-standing disciplines, and what's left is just what's left, rather than anything coherent uniting it. I think of myself as a political philosopher; I'm interested in the normative evaluation of political life and state institutions. And that's fairly strongly connected to moral philosophy. Moral philosophy, as Robert Nozick said, sets the boundaries of political philosophy.*

Brian Leiter: *This is a hard question. I can tell you what academic philosophy is, and it bears some relation to what philosophy has been historically. That is, philosophy is concerned with foundational or fundamental questions about the nature of everything else that human beings do: how we live, how we ought to live, what art is, what we know, whether we know anything, what science is, and so on. In that sense philosophy really is the most capacious of all the disciplines even* *if it isn't, as Kant thought, the queen of the sciences. But since we've just been talking about Nietzsche, we can't forget that there is a very different conception of what philosophers are. A philosopher for Nietzsche was an honorific. It refers to the person who creates or legislates value. It's the person who, to borrow an image from one of my colleagues at the University of Chicago, Judge Richard Posner, is a moral entrepreneur. It's a nice image. It's somebody who creates new ways of evaluating things—what's important, what's worthwhile—that changes how an entire culture or an entire people understand those things.*

Jerrold Levinson: *Oh, I didn't know you were going to ask me the really hard questions. I can tell a joke that says what philosophy is. A young man is going on a date and he asks his father for advice. 'Dad, I'm really nervous, what will I talk about in the dead spots?' The father says, 'Look son, there are the three Fs: there's Food, Family, and Filosophy.' So the son says, 'Okay, I'll remember that.' So he goes on a date and he's with the date in the car after dinner; and there's one of these lulls, and so he thinks what am I going to say, my teeth are clattering. Ah, I'll remember my father's advice. 'So Mary, do you like asparagus?' 'Well, no John I don't like asparagus.' 'Well, Mary, do you have any brothers?' 'Well actually John, I don't have any brothers.' 'Well, Mary, if you had a brother would he like asparagus?' That's philosophy.*

M. M. McCabe: *Thinking about thinking.*

Jeff McMahan: *Can I just laugh? I have no idea what philosophy is.*

Ray Monk: *Philosophy is the attempt to understand ourselves and the world.*

A. W. Moore: *I'm hard pressed to say, but one thing that is certainly true is that 'What is Philosophy?' is itself a striking philosophical question.*

Alexander Nehamas: *I can't answer that directly. I will tell you why I became a philosopher. I became a philosopher because I wanted to be able to talk about many, many things, ideally with knowledge, but sometimes not quite the amount of knowledge that I would need if I were to be a specialist in them. It allows you to be many different things. And plurality and complexity are very, very important to me.*

Alex Neill: *Philosophy is thinking that is obsessed with clarity.*

David Papineau: *Philosophy is thinking hard about the most difficult problems that there are. And you might think scientists do that too, but there's a certain kind of question whose difficulty can't be resolved by getting more empirical evidence. It requires an untangling of presuppositions: figuring out that our thinking is being driven by ideas we didn't even realize that we had. And that's what philosophy is.*

Anne Phillips: *Now I'm going to laugh. Philosophy for me is a way of thinking about dilemmas and contradictions. I don't think of it in terms of having to be abstracted from the real world, or having to be about hypothetical problems, but wherever you're dealing with something where there's a real dilemma and there are very good reasons to go one way, and very good reasons to go another, at that point I think you need philosophy.*

Thomas Pogge: *I think that philosophy in the classical sense is the love of wisdom. So the question then is 'What is wisdom?' And I think wisdom is understanding what really matters in the world. And that's* *how I would answer people who say what I'm doing is not really philosophy. In my view what really matters is the enormous injustice that's being perpetrated on the poor in this world. We have just heard from the food and agricultural organization of the United Nations that for the first time in human history there are more than a billion people who are chronically malnourished. The poorest half of humankind has 3 per cent of global household income: the richest half 97 per cent. If the poorest half had 4 per cent of global household income they wouldn't have this severe poverty. And what the philosopher can do is just to say, 'this is something that matters'.*

Janet Radcliffe Richards: *I regard philosophy as a mode of enquiry rather than a particular set of subjects. I regard it as involving the kind of questions where you're not trying to find out how your ideas latch on to the world, whether your ideas are true or not, in the way that science is doing, but more about how your ideas hang together. This means that philosophical questions will arise in a lot of subjects. And if you haven't got philosophical training you may well misunderstand the nature of a lot of those questions. So that's how I prefer to think of philosophy—as a method, a kind of enquiry rather than a particular set of questions. Although of course there are some questions that can only be answered by that sort of enquiry.*

Aaron Ridley: *(Laughs).*

Ben Rogers: *(Laughs). I must get back to the day job.*

Michael Sandel: *Philosophy is reflecting critically on the way things are. That includes reflecting critically on social and political and economic arrangements. It always intimates the possibility that things could be other than they are. And better.*

Julian Savulescu: *Philosophy is in my view gaining knowledge through the use of reason and conceptual tools, a priori reason, and by reflecting about oneself and the state of the world. It employs the empirical sciences, but it's not a version of science. It's gaining knowledge through rational reflection. And in my own area philosophy is about understanding what people should do, what sort of person people should be, how people should act, by rationally reflecting on the courses of action or the nature of human beings. I also think philosophy should encourage people to gain knowledge, and reflect and to try to seek to understand the world and themselves through their capacity as rational animals.*

Walter Sinnott-Armstrong: *Philosophy is the search for a coherent and justified overall world-view. Philosophers should stop looking at little issues in the corner of our lives and try to see how things fit together; how psychology fits with philosophy, how the mind fits with the body, how aesthetic value relates to economic value and justice. Those are the big issues: how do we fit together the different aspects of our lives? And that's what philosophy ought to be addressing.*

Barry Smith: *I think it's thinking fundamentally clearly and well about the nature of reality and our place in it, so as to understand better what goes on around us, and what our contribution is to that reality, and its effect on us.*

Robert Rowland Smith: *I think the Greek term has it exactly right; it's a way of loving knowledge.*

Paul Snowdon: *Philosophy is the name we give to a collection of questions which are of deep interest to us and for which there isn't any specialist way of answering. The categories in terms of which they are posed are ones which prevent experiments being carried out to answer them, so we're thrown back on trying to answer them on the basis of* *evidence we can accumulate. For example, 'Does God exist?' You can't hand that question over to some chap in a white coat to do an experiment. The category 'God' isn't a category suitable for conducting experiments to determine whether there's something of that sort or not. How do we decide? Well we simply have to weigh up the arguments for and against the existence of this kind of entity. And that is the general character of philosophical questions. Do values exist? Does the soul exist? Do sense data exist? And so on. 'Philosophy' is the name for that group of deep and important questions where there is no simple experimental way of answering them, and yet we want to know the answers.*

Kate Soper: *I think that one of the important things that philosophy is trying to do is to respect both the cultural relativity and historicity of our ideas while at the same time tease out what might be more trans-historical, trans-cultural truths.*

Raymond Tallis: *One of my favourite definitions comes from Wilfrid Sellars. It is trying to see how things in the wider sense hang together in the wider sense. And my dream of philosophy is to make the universe we live in mind-portable, so instead of being possessed by it, you possess it.*

Tzvetan Todorov: *Philosophy is a subject that all French students have to take in the last class of high school. And they just hate it, because they can't understand what philosophy is about. To answer more seriously, philosophy was a way of searching for wisdom, of leading a wiser life. And I adhere to this conception of philosophy.*

Keith Ward: *I have a traditional, almost Indian approach to this: I think philosophy is the pursuit of wisdom, and that includes spiritual wisdom. So this means asking questions about the nature of the human self and the nature of reality, and how this will affect your life in* *practice. And in that sense, although I have experienced Oxford philosophy at its most intense, I'm definitely not an ordinary language philosopher.*

Jonathan Wolff: *Well, I can tell you how philosophical problems arise in my view, which is where two common-sense notions push in different directions, and then philosophy gets started. And I suppose I also think that anything that claims to be philosophy which can't be related back to a problem that arises in that way probably is empty.*

ETHICS

I

JULIAN SAVULESCU ON
'Yuk!'

David Edmonds: *Is there any word more onomatopoeic than 'Yuk!'?
'Yuk!' expresses repugnance, disgust, abhorrence. The thought of a
genetically tampered-with mouse with a human ear on its back evokes, in
many people, a sense of Yuk! The idea of eating a human corpse draws the
same response. But how much weight should we give to these feelings of Yuk!
when we're trying to work out what's right and wrong? Julian Savulescu is
Director of Oxford University's Uehiro Centre for Practical Ethics.*

Nigel Warburton: *The topic we're going to focus on is 'Yuk!' or the
'Yuk!' factor. Could you just say what that means? What is the 'Yuk!'
factor?*

Julian Savulescu: Everyone is familiar with disgusting taste,
you taste something extremely bitter and you go 'Yuk!' But
in many cases we see or think about some particular ethical
issue and we have exactly the same disgust response. Typical

examples are when people think about cannibalism, about abortion, incest, or even having sex with animals: people have intuitive feelings of revulsion or disgust to those sorts of practices.

NW: *These reactions are pretty widespread; is there some biological explanation of why we should have such feelings?*

JS: Many of us are familiar with having disgust reactions. If you ever had food-poisoning—I had food-poisoning from some sausages once and I always felt sick when I thought about eating sausages, I couldn't eat them for many years— and many of these disgust reactions are evolutionarily programmed in order to protect us from toxins or adverse situations. For example, the revulsion to incest has a very good biological reason; you're much more likely to have a genetically abnormal child with a relative. So, many of the taboos have a strong biological basis; if you like, a quasi-rational basis. Some of them embody a kind of intuitive social form of knowledge, of practices that we've found in the past to be disadvantageous to human beings. So, our disgust reaction represents the expression of that knowledge.

NW: *So what you're saying is that there is more than one type of 'Yuk!' reaction, sometimes it's genetics; or sometimes as with your sausages you have a bad experience and thereafter you're afraid of sausages—so that's a learnt reaction.*

JS: It can also be learnt at a social level and it can be passed on through generations via a social form of knowledge. Many of the taboos and norms are socially determined from practices that were disadvantageous to groups. So, there are some very good bases for our 'Yuk!' reactions. But in many cases, they either express a personal disgust or misfire in the sense that they are applied to a situation that is no longer disadvantageous to us. As I said, my reaction to sausages persisted long after there were safe sausages available.

For example, with incest, we now have very good genetic tests that would pick up genetic abnormality. So, if *that* was the basis for the adverse reaction to incest, we can now in modern society counter that. The challenge of modern ethics today is not simply to sit with our intuitions, because our intuitions are not necessarily reliable guides to what we should do. We need to examine what we should do and what our reasons for actions are in a particular case. Take an example: many people would have a 'Yuk!' reaction to creating human or non-human animals, chimeras or hybrids. They have visions of planet of the apes or the chimeras of antiquity, the centaur, the sphinx, and so on.

But when we're considering what science is actually proposing, of creating embryos as a source of stem cells, and where those embryos would be destroyed after fourteen days, we need to look at what the reasons specifically are for that particular practice. We can't simply look at our 'Yuk!' reactions. They are very crude rules of thumb that have served us in our primitive past, but are simply ill-equipped to deal with complexities and the nuances of particular situations in today's life.

NW: *What would you say to somebody who says, 'Look, actually our reason-giving is pretty crude, too. It's a kind of rationalization after the fact; most people end up rationalizing their deepest prejudices and probably their "Yuk!" reactions at some level'?*

JS: That's a very good point. Many people do use ethical arguments simply to rationalize their intuitive responses. A famous psychologist, Jonathan Haidt, used a scenario around incest where he kept probing participants in the experiment for their reason for their objections. Whatever reasons they offered, whether it was genetic disability or harm to other members of the family, or paedophilia, he countered these reasons by saying the situation won't be like that, and he went on to give an explanation why not. However, they stuck to their intuitive objection to it, regardless of how invalid their supposed reason was. In the end, they couldn't offer any other reasons, except that they intuitively had a 'Yuk!' reaction to it. So, there's certainly that phenomenon.

But secular ethics, not ethics based on religious codes, is only half-a-century old really. The challenge is to find reasons that aren't just intuitive. So, reasons to do with people's well-being or reasons to do with rights, or reasons to do with freedom, are reasons that aren't just based on our intuitions; we think that there's something more substantial behind those sorts of values. So the challenge is to find values that aren't just grounded on individual feelings but are grounded on some ethical principle or value that's defensible.

NW: *Yet when it comes to ethics committees, quite often things I've read are basically 'Yuk!' reactions. They say, 'Well, that's just disgusting. That's a kind of Frankenstein approach'—a whole lot of trigger words that seem to be synonyms for 'I find that repugnant'.*

JS: That's certainly correct. Much ethical discourse still operates at a fairly intuitive primitive level. We saw this in the 1950s or '60s with the debate around homosexuality:

many people thought that this threatened the moral fabric of society or that it was just disgusting and that homosexuality should never be legalized. Fortunately we moved ahead of that when we found we couldn't find good reasons to create or to sustain a legal ban on homosexuality within the privacy of people's homes. That's been a good thing and a triumph for ethical thought and reason over emotions, because the sorts of arguments that were provided there probably had some evolutionary basis, they probably did express some attitudes that had served us in the past, but simply had no place in modern society.

We resolve these issues through rational discourse, through examining our emotional reactions and our intuitions, and we attempt to provide reasons for our policies and that's how it should be. We should strive to do that better, rather than descending to a kind of democratic approach to ethics where we take a vote as to how people respond, how much 'Yuk!' there is out there in a population towards that particular practice.

NW: *Emotions are obviously very important in our moral behaviour; some people might caricature our discussion so far as, you are simply defending the power of reason. But where does emotion come in if it doesn't come in through these powerful intuitions?*

JS: In many circumstances we have to think quickly and we have to rely on rough rules of thumb: so we have to rely on our immediate emotional responses. Sometimes they help us to act quickly and accurately in complex situations; in some circumstances, they provide a guide to actions; in some cases, it's important to have certain emotional reactions in certain social circumstances. So if somebody threatens you, it might be important to get angry in order to respond in the right way: it might not be the right thing to turn the other cheek. Lastly, emotions are probably the most important part of our lives, so how we feel about things is incredibly important. We have to take account of that in deciding what the best course of action is.

But ethics is not just emotions: at some point we have to stand above them and critically reflect. I was originally a doctor, and everyone feels revulsion when they have to see a termination of pregnancy. It's a natural human response. There would be something abnormal with you if you were a human who didn't have that sort of emotional response to the destruction of human life. But does that mean we can settle the issue of whether abortion is right or wrong by looking at how we feel about it? I don't think so.

NW: *Does it follow from what you're saying that all of us should critically examine our own 'Yuk!' reactions, to see where our particular biases lie in this respect?*

JS: I think we should start by acknowledging how we feel about situations and understand why we feel that way about them. But we should seek to reflect on that and decide whether there are reasons that overcome our feelings and direct us to some other course of action. My father died in hospital and I've seen autopsies performed and I didn't want him to have an autopsy after his death. But after reflecting, I asked for an autopsy report because I thought it was important that we understood why he died. So, I think it's important in our lives to go one step beyond just acknowledging our feelings and ask: 'Are there are any good reasons for or against that course of action that may differ from how we feel about it?'

NW: *Are there any particular moral issues of the day at the moment which would benefit from a kind of cleansing of this 'Yuk!' vocabulary?*

JS: I think issues to do with changing human biology and human nature and radical advances in biological science are something that we're going to have to really go beyond appealing to our 'Yuk!' reactions, because what's on offer is enormous. The advances of human biology could provide fundamental improvements to the human condition and human nature. But many people have a 'Yuk!' response to changing human nature. They have ideas of us playing God, of us creating Frankenstein, of us creating human devils. But what's really on offer is the ability to unshackle ourselves from our evolutionary constraints. Evolution was simply concerned with creating beings that live long enough to reproduce. Yet we care much more about other aspects of our lives than simply whether we can reproduce. Our fundamental cognitive abilities, our physical abilities, even our capacity to love other people could be influenced by changes in human biology.

We now understand the patterns of human relationships and love. We understand there are three phases: lust, attraction, attachment, each with different hormonal mechanisms, each of which can be manipulated or influenced in certain ways, strategically and scientifically. Instead of falling out of love we could maintain love through the use of biology. In terms of physical enhancements, scientists have created a mouse that can run 5 kilometres on a treadmill at 20 metres per minute; the normal mouse runs 200 metres, not 5 kilometres. The mouse lives longer and reproduces much longer, it's much healthier. We could make the same genetic changes in humans. So we'll have to ask whether we can simply settle these questions by looking at our intuitions and our 'Yuk!' reactions—I don't think so. There will be good reasons against them, but those reasons won't be generated by simplistic appeals to our intuitions or to our 'Yuk!' reactions.

NW: *Is there a danger that if we rid ourselves of the 'Yuk!' reaction that we'll be vulnerable to certain sorts of systematic biases in reasoning that we all know exist?*

JS: One of the standard objections that you hear is that this is precisely what the Nazis did, they overcame their 'Yuk!' reactions to killing human beings, and look what happened there. It's really a bad analogy, because the Nazis couldn't appeal to any sort of fundamental values that we all share, and I don't think the fact that they were able to overcome their emotional reactions was the fundamental problem. What we need are sound ethical principles. You've got to remember the people who kept slaves, who stopped women voting, believed that they were doing the right thing, had 'Yuk!' reactions to blacks marrying whites—and very profound, very deep, very widespread emotions; they were certain that their intuitions were correct.

NW: *Is there anything that you still find completely repugnant even though reason says this shouldn't be absolutely immoral to pursue?*

JS: Yes, I have that reaction to having sex with animals. You could justify it if it were the case that the animal and the human were both enjoying it and it didn't cause further harm to anyone else. I can't see any very strong reason against it except that it's a waste of time: you could do better things with your time. But I still have quite a strong emotional reaction to it. It's not something I'd want to find out that my children were engaged in. I guess the other one is the German cannibalism case, where one person wanted to be eaten and the other one wanted to eat him. I still feel fairly revolted by that idea, even if we can't find strong reasons against it.

2

SIMON BLACKBURN ON
Relativism

David Edmonds: *What's ethically acceptable for Muslims may not be acceptable for Christians. What's seen as morally acceptable in Manchester may not be alright in Mogadishu. You may think capital punishment or euthanasia is wrong: I may disagree. We're tempted to think that morality is relative—that we can resolve moral disputes as we resolve disputes in other areas. In history, say, we might argue about the date of the Battle of Hastings; in maths we might challenge a proof—but we think there's a definitive answer to such disagreements. Which raises the question—is the realm of morality different, are morals relative? The man to answer this question is one of Britain's leading moral philosophers, Professor Simon Blackburn.*

Nigel Warburton: *The topic I want to discuss is moral relativism. Could you sketch out what you understand by that term?*

Simon Blackburn: Moral relativism is a position that intrigues even if it doesn't attract people. It starts with the elementary observation that there are different sensibilities—people react differently, morally, to different things. Some people think abortion is permissible, others think it's not. Some people think that assisted euthanasia is permissible, others think it isn't. Some people think the will of Allah has to be done, other people don't think it's of any relevance. So you have different views, different positions, and the potential for conflict, obviously. The question then arises, can we defend the idea of one single moral truth in the face of all this diversity? Or is the diversity a sign that there isn't really a single moral truth, rather as people think, in matters of taste, that there isn't a single truth?

NW: *In the area of taste people frequently say, 'It's all subjective'. What you've described sounded like what's often called subjectivism. Do you see subjectivism as a variety of relativism or the core of it?*

SB: It's a variety of it. The subjectivist is a relativist because he will think as the relativist does that I can say truly that abortion is permissible, let's say, and you can say truly that it's not, and we each have our own truth. And the subjectivist protects that idea by saying 'I'm describing my own reaction. I'm saying of myself that I approve of abortion, and you're saying of yourself that you don't. And then those two remarks are compatible, they could each be true. Just as I like toothpaste with a mint flavour, and you don't.'

NW: *So relativism would be any theory which encapsulates the idea that there are individual differences in morality (for which there may be a cultural explanation) and that there are no absolute truths about any moral judgements that we make. The statement 'Torturing babies is wrong' is subjective; it's just a matter of taste.*

SB: That's pretty much it, yes. That's a very good thumbnail definition. As the example of subjectivism shows, it can then be worked out in various ways. But the core idea has to remain that I've got my truth, you've got your truth, and there's no metaphysical—or absolute, as you put it—norm or value knocking about in the universe that I'm getting right and you're getting wrong or vice versa.

NW: *So is it true? Is moral relativism actually an accurate picture of the nature of morality?*

SB: I argue no, it's not true. The reason it's not true is that it doesn't do justice to the fact of disagreement and conflict. That is, if I think that abortion is right or permissible and you think it never is, we've got a disagreement, and it's a disagreement that could lead to conflict, and in serious cases moral disagreement can lead to war. That's not like 'I like mint toothpaste' and 'I don't' in different mouths where you just say 'Okay, sure, live and let live, *de gustibus non est disputandum*'.[1] You just can't say that in the moral case. If I think that fox-hunting with dogs is absolutely wrong, and you think that it's an admirable part of English country life, then we've got a political disagreement on our hands. The relativist doesn't do justice to that because he says 'you've got your truth and I've got mine'—end of story. But the trouble is, it's not the end of the story because we're each seeking to impose a policy on the other.

NW: *In some cases where there is disagreement, there are facts which, if they become known, resolve the issue. Is that what you're saying morality is like?*

[1] (Latin) 'There's no disputing about taste.'

SB: Well, not quite. My position gets rather complicated here. There are, for example, people called 'moral realists' who think there must be a fact: either fox-hunting is right or it's not right and it's our job to find out which. And they see that as a kind of metaphysical commitment: there's a moral reality and their problem is making sense of that. I take a more pragmatic view. I say, look, whether or not there's such a moral reality—and let's just shunt that to one side for the moment—we're going to have disagreement, we're going to have conflict and we're going to need to know what to do—we're going perhaps to be conflicted in our own minds about things: should I allow my teenage son or daughter to do this, that, or the other? That's got nothing to do with the attempt to get a moral reality right. It has everything to do with an attempt to work out how to live, to work out a plan or a scheme for living. And I think it's the same with more serious moral disagreements. So I would defend the practical importance of thinking about ethics on pragmatic grounds, not on the grounds that we're attempting to describe a moral reality which is a rather mysterious, ontological denizen of the universe.

NW: *A moral relativist would probably say that female circumcision is acceptable for certain cultural groups: it's right for them, it's wrong for us. That doesn't give any clue as to how you might resolve the conflict between those two different groups, how you would apply the pragmatic idea faced with a cultural relativist like that.*

SB: Well, often the kind of remark you just cited is a plea for live and let live, or toleration, or possibly even an injunction that we have no right to interfere, we mustn't interfere, there's something wrong about imposing our will on other people. I think that's only partially true. It's sometimes true that we shouldn't impose our will. But in some cases I'm not sure it's true at all. For example, the female-circumcision case, where I think it's quite legitimate for people to feel that the treatment is so degrading and so misogynistic in various ways and does such damage to people that we do become very uncomfortable about just standing aside and letting it happen.

NW: *There's a famous knock-down argument against the kind of moral relativism that we've been discussing. This is that most moral relativists believe absolutely that relativism is true, so they're inconsistent in some way: they both believe that every judgement is relative, but also that the judgement 'every judgement is relative' is itself absolutely true, so not relative.*

SB: Yes, that's a very good old argument. It's the so-called 'Peritrope' of Plato from the *Theaetetus*. I think it's a doubtful argument myself. It's too quick. And the obvious response is for the relativist to say: 'Look, I don't put forward, for example, non-toleration or even my own relativism, as an absolute position, I don't believe in absolute positions, I just told you I think everything is relative. So I'm quite happy to admit that status for my own position. That means it's no better or worse than other things. But then you have to take it as it appears to you. And my persuasive ambition is to persuade you that the right way to think about it is that everything is relative.'

NW: *So how would you characterize your own position? What name is it usually known by?*

SB: It's an unlovely title that I landed myself with, but it has stuck. I'm called a quasi-realist. And what that suggests is that, without going metaphysical—as I say, I don't believe with starting with the idea of a moral reality—it is justifiable to talk in terms of disagreement, in terms of attempts to find solutions, attempts to come to one mind and to worry how I'm to live my life. All those are genuine concerns, and genuine phenomena. And the relativist is really trying to undermine something in our practices, and I want to defend our practices. I want to defend the seriousness with which we take moral disagreement and try to resolve it. So it's 'as if' you've got a moral reality which it is our job to find, although that picture is, I think, only a picture.

NW: *Take the debate about multiculturalism—a major issue in Britain. Some people say that toleration has gone too far, that what we've been doing is tolerating many intolerant people, with devastating results. Does your approach have anything to say about multiculturalism?*

SB: I don't think it directly speaks to it. But my approach would be very hospitable to the possibility that we've gone too far. Do we allow people complete licence in modes of behaviour or modes of speech or do we clamp down? Obviously the pendulum can swing—you can go far too far in either direction. And equally obviously, it's a complicated matter of political judgement, whether at any particular time we've gone too far one way or too far the other.

NW: *And do you think philosophers have got anything that they can add to that debate, or are they just commentating on the sidelines, like sports commentators?*

SB: I do rather tend to the second view. Although I believe wholeheartedly in the practice of moral debate, and I think there are very serious questions we have to tackle, like, for example, the limits of toleration, I'm rather sceptical about the existence of expertise, or expertise across the board. There are things philosophers can bring to the debate. Traditional virtues of clarity and care, knowing when it's an empirical problem, knowing when it's a moral disagreement, and things like that. But I do jib at the idea of moral expertise. And certainly, if you come to the philosopher for solutions in any moderately complicated political arena, you'll just find that you've got a dozen philosophers and thirteen solutions, as they say about economists. That's a result of the fact that, fundamentally, morality is a deep expression of personality, and of plans for living, plans for the body politic that we admire—and people will differ. So we go back to the relativist starting-point—people will differ.

NW: *You've described yourself as a quasi-realist and said that although debates on moral issues are real debates at some level there's no objective truth about how they should be resolved. How, then, do you explain how these moral disagreements are genuine disagreements?*

SB: Well, at one level that's quite easy. Take a non-moral case. Suppose we have to decide where to go on holiday and you say 'let's go to the mountains' and I say 'let's go to the seaside'. Then we've got a disagreement, and it's a real disagreement, assuming we can only go to one, and we have either to bargain, or negotiate, or work through it, and give each other reasons for preferring the one to the other. And of course eventually it could lead to conflict or, in the case of partners, divorce. So in practical matters, just as much as in theoretical matters, disagreement is very often the name of the game. Similarly, if I want people to go on fox-hunting and you want them not to, then just at the level of desire we've got a disagreement and you could be expected to act to prevent fox-hunting and I act to promote it. We've got policies that are in conflict and we might come to blows, as people do. So disagreement is not too problematic, and if you see the relativist as trying to somehow wish it away, then the position does begin to look silly, impractical. Suppose you say 'Fox-hunting Yes!' and I say 'Fox-hunting No!', and in comes Rosy The Relativist, and she says 'Hey you two, why don't you just realize that fox-hunting is good for Nigel and bad for Simon and that's the end of it?' The question I want to ask is, 'How does this help?' Whatever led me to oppose fox-hunting is presumably still there; whatever led you to admire it or wish to tolerate it is still there. The idea that we're not in conflict just starts to look farcical. And the conflict has not been resolved by Rosy—it hasn't even been helped.

3

PETER SINGER ON
Animals

David Edmonds: *In 1975* Animal Liberation *was published: in hindsight, a seminal work of philosophy, marking the birth of the modern animal rights movement—though its author spoke not of rights per se, but, as a utilitarian, in terms, put crudely, of maximizing interests or happiness. The Australian author is now at Princeton and arguably the world's most famous philosopher. He believes that some animals have a higher moral status than some humans and that our disregard for animal suffering is a deplorable moral blind spot. He also has contentious views on euthanasia, abortion, on infanticide, on civil disobedience, and on how much we should give to charity. But we spoke to Peter Singer about how humans treat animals.*

Nigel Warburton: *The topic we're going to focus on is the ethics of using animals, both as food and in research. Before we start, it's probably best to get clear about what you understand by a 'person', because you distinguish a 'person' from a 'human being'.*

Peter Singer: A person is someone who is aware of their own existence over time, aware enough to realize that they're the same being who lived previously and who can expect to live into the future. So most human beings are persons, but none of us was born a person. Newborn infants are not persons. And some non-human animals are persons, but not all non-human animals are persons.

NW: *So what kind of non-human animal might be a person?*

PS: A chimpanzee, for example, is probably aware of its own existence over time. So I think there's good evidence that chimpanzees are persons.

NW: *What about adult humans who lack the mental capacity to think about their own past as their own. Would they not be persons?*

PS: I think they're no longer persons. They may have been persons, and we may choose to respect the wishes they had when they were persons. But there comes a time—at least if the body outlives your intellectual capacities to such an extent that you can no longer be aware of your past or even the idea that you have a future—when you would cease to be a person.

NW: *Somebody reading this who is not a philosopher will say 'Well look, you can define a person, you can define a human being, so what?'*

PS: Absolutely, that's quite the right reaction. Definitions don't show anything, normatively. But I think the idea of a being who can envisage his or her own future is morally significant, because if you compare the wrongness of killing a being who is capable of having some anticipation of the future, some desires for the future, perhaps even some projects to complete in the future, and you kill such a person who wants to go on living, you're doing something wrong to that person which is something you're not doing if you kill a being who is not fully a person and who can have no wishes or hopes for the future which could be cut off or thwarted or frustrated. So the concept of the person points to something that is relevant in the specific context of the wrongness of killing.

NW: *To me, the real issue with animals is whether they suffer or not. All kinds of animals are capable of suffering even if they don't have a conception of their life continuing.*

PS: I totally agree. You brought up the topic of persons, not me. The major issue about animals and how we treat them is that they're capable of suffering. I don't think it's about the wrongness of killing them.

NW: *It's interesting that many of your critics focus on descriptions of a situation where you're playing off a human being who's less than a person against an animal which is a person.*

PS: I think that's a tactic. It's quite an effective tactic with some audiences. They caricature my views by saying that, on my view, animals deserve more consideration than humans do. I don't think that is true in general, although it is true that there are some rare situations where a human is so intellectually disabled or incapable of understanding things that I would, other things being equal, give preference to the non-human animal. The animal could then have a greater interest in going on living, or in not suffering in a certain way. But that's really completely irrelevant to the vast majority of cases in which we are interfering with animals, for example, when we're producing them for food in factory farms. Then it's not even necessary for me to say that they have the same status—let alone a superior status—to humans. All I need to do is point to the fact that we're inflicting unnecessary suffering on them. That should be enough to show that what we are doing is wrong, given that we're not doing this in order to save human lives but just because we like to eat a certain kind of food.

NW: *Another concept that's important in your work is 'speciesism', the idea that it's somehow akin to racism to treat other animals, non-human animals, in a way that we wouldn't treat human beings.*

PS: It's not so much that we're treating animals in a way we wouldn't treat human beings. Because sometimes that may be appropriate, given that they have different interests, different capacities. Sometimes we should treat them differently, just as we sometimes quite properly treat small children differently from the way we treat older human beings. The point about speciesism is that we give less weight to the interests of beings who are not members of our species simply because they are not members of our species. We are not looking at their individual characteristics, nor at their capacities, or what's good for them, or bad for them. We just say: 'Well, they're not members of the species *Homo sapiens*, therefore we can use them for our purposes, our ends; we don't have to treat them as if their ends mattered.' Whereas if we are dealing with a human being, no matter what the mental level of that human being, we say that that human being's life is sacred, he or she is an end in itself, we must respect the dignity of that human being, and so on.

That's speciesism—just to take the species in itself as determinative of moral status.

NW: *But isn't that simply a good rule of thumb? When you see another person, you tend to think of them evolving over time, with a sense of themselves and a capacity to feel pain, in a way that a fish, like a haddock say, doesn't.*

PS: Well, for one thing not all of our encounters with animals are with haddock. For another, while I agree with the first part of what you said, that the human is likely to have more of a self-conception, more of an awareness of itself as existing over time, than an animal, I'm not so clear that human beings are going to have a greater capacity to suffer. We know that non-human animals have some senses that are more acute than ours. Eagles have better eyesight, dogs have a better sense of smell, and so on. It's not at all impossible that because of their need to live in sharp contact with the world animals have capacities to feel pain that are just as acute or more acute than ours. We shouldn't take it as a rule of thumb that humans always suffer more than animals, and certainly not that human suffering matters more, which is really the point about speciesism.

NW: *Now, the two main ways in which many of us use animals are as food, or in some kind of experimentation, possibly for scientific research, possibly research in cosmetics. You're a utilitarian; that is, you're interested in maximizing happiness in some sense, or maximizing the interests of sentient beings—and that's how we can tell whether something is right or wrong.*

PS: That's correct: whether, all things considered and in the long run, you've done what's best in the interests of, or will best satisfy the preferences of, all sentient beings.

NW: *But doesn't this just complicate everything? Most of us, most of the time are most interested in other human beings. If you start including all kinds of animals, how do you work out what to do?*

PS: It does complicate things. Just as, if you're a white European in the eighteenth century, it complicated things to have to consider the interests of Africans. That interferes with your profitable trade in slaves. But even though it's more complicated, it's still something we ought to do. Now it is true that the calculations can't be done with any precision at all, but in some situations we can make rough comparisons and sometimes it's pretty clear that we're inflicting more suffering than is justified by the benefit that we're getting out of it. One of those situations is factory farming.

In factory farming, we confine animals in conditions that for their entire lives make them miserable. They can't satisfy their basic needs, neither physically in terms of moving around, exercising, having comfortable bedding, nor socially and psychologically in terms of mixing with the right kind of social groups suited for their species. Laying hens might be suffering for their entire lives. Breeding sows might be in stalls too narrow for them even to turn around, let alone walk, for most of their lives.

We have to ask: what do we get out of this? Well, we produce food a little more cheaply. But we are not starving, and we can afford to pay a little more for our food. I don't think there's much doubt that that's not something that can be justified if we give equal consideration to the sufferings of the hens and the pigs.

NW: *But isn't that just an argument for eating free-range meat rather than factory-farm meat?*

PS: It's an argument that says, a clear-cut case of something wrong that we do to animals is factory farming. You were asking about how we make complicated comparisons across species, and so I answered that factory farming is something that we can definitely say is not justified. That's not to say that if you get into other forms of farming you may not still find things that are undesirable and you might still reasonably come to the conclusion that we shouldn't be doing that. But the case against these other forms of raising animals will not be as black-and-white as the case against factory farming.

NW: *And if you take the example of eating game—animals that have lived in the wild that have been killed very quickly, with gunshot perhaps—that, presumably, is more morally acceptable than eating free-range meat which has to be taken to be slaughtered?*

PS: I think that's generally true. It will depend on the particular circumstances, including how reliably you can put a bullet through the brain of an animal and kill it instantly rather than have it wounded and escaping. But if you are a good shot in an area with ecologically sustainable hunting, it's better to go hunting for your meat than to go down to a supermarket for it.

NW: *What I like about what you're saying is that it's so reasoned. Everything is consistent; you're looking for an argument that makes*

distinctions based not on how you feel about killing or animal suffering,
but about what the implications are, rationally. Most people I've met
who are vegetarians have a complete sense of revulsion about eating
meat, or harming animals in any way, which they might not be able to
justify rationally. So perhaps they're not moral vegetarians?

PS: Some of them may be aesthetic vegetarians: that is, they
are repulsed by the idea of killing an animal. And I agree that
there is something that does repel me about it. Even if I
convince myself by the argument that we were just having
that in certain circumstances it's acceptable to shoot deer, I
still wouldn't like the idea of watching that beautiful animal
suddenly drop dead and be reduced to a carcass and a piece of
meat. But speaking as a moral philosopher I have to consider
whether this is just a 'Yuk!' response that we might have to
other things that actually are quite defensible or justifiable,
or whether there's a serious ethical reason for not doing it.

NW: *So do you believe that we should all be vegetarians?*

PS: Almost all, I would say. If there is somebody who is
living a traditional indigenous life, whether it's an Inuit who
survives by killing fish, or Australian aboriginals who are
still living a traditional life that might involve occasionally
killing some animals, I would not presume to say to them
that they have to abandon their way of life and go and live in
a city where they can earn money and buy their food in a
supermarket. That's a somewhat different situation from our
own.

NW: *So in a sense, those who aren't vegetarians are immoral to a*
degree. But how immoral is it to eat meat?

PS: Compared to what? Yes, it's normally morally wrong. None of us is perfect, though. I don't consider everything I do is perfect, but I think part of living a morally good life is having concern for the consequences of what you do. That includes having concern for animals who are affected by your actions. These things suggest that most people in developed nations—where they have a wide choice of nutritious food and can easily nourish themselves well without eating meat—would be living a better life if they were vegetarian.

NW: *For me that's a very classical conception of philosophy—that you don't just think it, you live it.*

PS: Absolutely. I wouldn't still be doing moral philosophy if I thought it was just a theoretical game. When I was a teenager I was fascinated by chess, and I used to spend time looking at chess problems, 'white to move and mate in two', that sort of thing. It was fun and intellectually stimulating, but I wouldn't want to spend my life doing it. There are things that are more important. And sometimes I think people doing philosophy almost reduce it to the level of solving chess puzzles.

NW: *I live in Oxford, where there's a large building just been built specifically to do research on animals. That's another way in which animals are frequently used and that causes them suffering. But it's defended in terms of the outcome. There are other ways of surviving because you could be a vegetarian. But how could you do medical research without doing animal experimentation?*

PS: There's plenty of medical research being done without animal experimentation. A lot of medical research is done through trials with humans, and we've also greatly increased the amount of research we can do using tissue cultures (the growth of tissues and/or cells separate from the organism), computer simulations, and various other alternatives to using animals. This area of animal research has grown over the last thirty years, partly as a result of pressure from the animal movement, and that's a very good thing. But I'm not going to say that there's nothing we can learn from research using animals.

NW: *So you're not an absolutist. You think there are situations in which it could be morally acceptable to use non-human animals for the benefit of human beings?*

PS: It could be. I certainly couldn't rule that out as a theoretical possibility. But I would have a very high bar to be cleared before you could go ahead and do that. And one of the reasons I would have a very high bar is that I think the whole institutional practice of research on animals has grown up with the speciesist prejudice that I mentioned before: that animals really don't count, or not very much anyway. And, therefore, for many medical researchers, it's not a problem to say 'Get me fifty rats' or 'Get me twenty dogs'.

That's why I don't want to justify the general practice of animal experimentation and I certainly don't want to justify or defend what happens in the building you described, a building that I know is very controversial in Oxford. Because I expect what is going on there is that scientists are carrying on their business as usual in which the interests of animals are not given anything like the weight that the interests of humans at comparable mental levels would be given.

NW: *When you started writing about the suffering of animals, speciesism, and so on, that was a very radical position to take. Things have evolved since then. There are many more people who go along with your reasoning. Do you think there will be a time in the future when people will look back and say 'I can't believe they were eating meat, I can't believe they did experiments on chimpanzees'?*

PS: I hope so. At least I am fairly sure they'll say: 'I can't believe they were locking animals up in factory farms so they didn't have room to walk around or turn around.' And I do hope they'll say: 'I can't believe what they were doing to chimpanzees.' Indeed, we've almost got to that point now with chimpanzees. You look back on some of the things that were done not that long ago, twenty or thirty years ago, and people are quite horrified that those experiments were permitted. So we are making progress. I very much hope that we will continue to do so.

4

MICHAEL SANDEL ON
Sport and Enhancement

David Edmonds: *The science of genetics is advancing faster than our moral intuitions can cope. No longer are so-called 'Designer Babies' just a figment of the imagination, restricted to the realm of sci-fi movies. The implications are huge—and not just for babies and reproduction. We can modify our genetic make-up as adults too. Take sport: in theory we can now manipulate genes to make athletes run faster, jump higher, throw further. Does that mean sport will evolve into a form of competition between quasi-robots? And if so, would it matter? The distinguished and genetically unmodified Harvard philosopher Michael Sandel believes that we should be extremely cautious in our attempts to shape and master nature, and indeed to master our shape.*

Nigel Warburton: *The topic we're going to focus on is genetic enhancement, specifically enhancement in the area of sport. Could you sketch the kinds of enhancements that are possible now and some that will be possible in the near future using genetic techniques?*

Michael Sandel: As far as sports are concerned, we hear a lot about blood doping and the use of steroids for performance enhancement in athletes. In the not-distant future it will be possible to use various forms of gene therapy, for example, to enhance muscle, and that I think is what in the area of sport will raise the most difficult questions.

NW: *Could you give us some general pointers as to why you're against enhancement?*

MS: I should first clarify that I'm in favour of the use of biotechnology for medical purposes for the sake of health. So, for example, vaccination—vaccination against smallpox, for example—enhances the immune system. I'm all for that, because it promotes health. So any use of new genetic technologies to repair injury or to cure or prevent disease I'm all in favour of.

What I've criticized is the use of bio-medical technologies not for medical purposes but for non-medical enhancements: for performance enhancement in athletes, to try to select the genetic traits of children, to try to enhance memory, to enhance height, let's say among children—who may be perfectly healthy but want to be taller, or their parents want them to be taller—sex selection: these are the kinds of non-medical uses of genetic engineering that I've criticized.

NW: *Quite central to your discussion here is the difference between a cure for something which is a deficiency and an enhancement that takes us beyond what's normal.*

MS: Yes, and I'll quickly acknowledge that there can be hard cases, right at the boundary. What about braces for orthodontia, for example? Is that related to health or is it merely cosmetic; is it just to improve one's bite or is it to fit a certain look that's become widespread in our society?

That would be an example of a hard case. But the underlying difference between a cure and a non-medical enhancement requires a normative idea of health and of human flourishing. Health is about restoring or preserving normal human faculties which are a constitutive ingredient but a very limited part of the good life.

NW: *In sport, enhancement is the name of the game. That's what most athletes want to do: to enhance performance. And they're prepared to do anything within the law, and often things which are pushing at the edge or going beyond the law. How could you persuade an athlete that they shouldn't be using enhancement?*

MS: There are two obvious arguments. One is safety: steroids, for example, have long-term medical risks. A second familiar reason is fairness. If there is a general ban in the Olympics on various forms of enhancement or blood doping or various forms of muscle enhancement, then if some use it surreptitiously or illicitly it puts the others at a disadvantage. But safety and fairness are not the only reasons to oppose genetic enhancement in sport.

NW: *In your book* The Case Against Perfection *you use the example of Tiger Woods, who allegedly had his eyesight dramatically improved from myopia to very good vision by laser technology. Now that seems to be perfectly acceptable: he could have worn glasses and achieved a similar sort of effect. Why is that alright, but an enhancement beyond that not?*

MS: Besides safety and fairness, my main objection to the use of performance-enhancing genetic therapies, for example, has to do with the worry that it will corrupt sport and

31

athletic competition as a place where we admire the cultivation and display of natural gifts. It will distance us from the human dimension of sport.

If you imagine a future where it's possible to engineer a bionic athlete, let's say in baseball, which is my favourite sport, who could hit every pitch for a home run of 600 feet. It would maybe be an amusing spectacle, but it wouldn't be a *sport*. We might admire the pharmacist or the engineer, but would we admire the athlete? We would lose contact with the human dimension and the display of natural human gifts that I think is essential to what we admire and appreciate in sports.

NW: *You could have a superb hitter, but what about a superb pitcher? And if you got those two together it seems to me that genetic enhancement would produce a wonderful sport. Just as with soccer, if you had a team in which every player was as good as Pelé, that would be wonderful to watch.*

MS: Would it? If we knew that all of the players were bionic athletes; robots, in effect, if you take it to the extreme? We might find it amusing to see robots or machines perform great athletic feats, but would we even consider them athletic feats or human athletic feats? There are technology-laden sports like auto-racing. I've never understood the appeal of auto-racing myself, but I think what makes it a sport or a game but not an athletic endeavour is that it's mainly the machines that we're watching, not the human excellence.

NW: *Well, take marathon running; that's a paradigm case of competitive athleticism. Any major athlete now who's a serious marathon* *runner will use all kinds of technological means to enhance their performance, and that doesn't detract from the sport. It's amazing to watch these people. People running sub-five-minute miles over and over again are almost a different species to me, but it's still wonderful to watch.*

MS: But we would still want to know what sort of training was enabling them to do that. And isn't there a difference between great training and ingesting a drug or going in for some kind of genetic therapy? Here's an extreme way of testing your idea about the marathon. It's true that new technologies do sometimes make for a better race; but that's because they bring out more fully the skills and the excellences that the best athletes display.

Once marathon runners ran barefoot. And then along came someone and invented a running-shoe. Some might have said that that corrupts the race. I think that's an enhancement that actually perfects rather than corrupts the race because it enables the race to be a better test of who's the best runner, removing contingencies like stepping on a sharp pebble.

Take another extreme case. In the Boston marathon some years ago the winner crossed the line first, was given her prize, but then it was discovered that she had used a rather unusual means of enhancement. After she got to the starting-line she hopped in the subway and rode it most of the way, got out, and ran across the finish-line. Now what is the difference between the running-shoe and the subway? Both are technologies that enhance the ability to create the race, but one of them corrupts the purpose of the sport. And that's the test we should use with new technologies.

NW: *I think there's an easy answer there, because the constitutive rules don't allow you to go on the subway; there's no rule on the running-shoes you can use, but there is on the mode of transport—apart from the shoes.*

MS: Appealing to the constitutive rules, if by that you mean the rules that happen to be set down by the governing body of the sport, won't be sufficient to answer the normative question—because we have to think about it from the standpoint of the people who are setting the rules. The Olympic Committee is trying to decide whether to permit runners and skiers to use a special oxygen chamber that runners might sleep in. The chamber enriches the red blood cells to enable the blood cells to carry more oxygen. The effect is the same as taking EPO, which is a hormone that increases the ability of the blood to carry oxygen, or blood doping. Both of these practices are illegal. So the question is: 'What should the rules be? Which technologies should the laws allow?' And for that we can't just appeal to the law.

NW: *Your argument relies on some idea of what is natural, and I'd like to hear what makes something natural. Because on one reading anything that a human being does is natural.*

MS: Right. And one could argue that the inventiveness that leads to the inventions of these biotechnologies is itself a natural human pursuit. That's true. My argument against enhancement, whether in the sports context or whether we're talking about creating designer children, is not to valorize or to sanctify nature as such. There are lots of things that are bad in nature: polio, for instance, or malaria. I'm all in favour of using biotechnology to banish those facts of nature. So the conception that I need to explain, what it is that troubles us about enhancement, has to do with the appreciation of the *gifted* character of human powers and talents and achievements: that not everything about us is at our disposal subject to our desire to master or dominate or manipulate nature. There is a certain hubris when human beings overreach and try to exert dominion over all of nature, including human nature. So I'm more worried about the human dispositions and the hubris that lies behind the drive to perfect our nature than I am concerned to sanctify or protect nature as such.

NW: *That notion of giftedness seems to imply somebody giving, and the obvious candidate is God. God 'gives us' certain natural attributes and it's for us to understand and develop those. But why would an atheist or an agnostic take your view on this seriously?*

MS: It's a very good question. I want to make the case that the ethic of giftedness can be supported by various religious views that see God as the giver, but that is not the only way of making sense of the idea of giftedness. We commonly speak of the athlete's 'gift' or the musician's 'gift', without necessarily attributing that gift to God. All the ethic of giftedness requires is an awareness, an appreciation, that not everything about us is the product of our own will, our own creation. It points to the moral importance of a certain attitude of restraint, even humility, in the face of what's been given to us. Some would say we should exercise that humility because to do otherwise would be to play God. But I think that humility in the face of the given can also be understood in secular terms.

NW: *And in the book you use three kinds of arguments against those who think we should master anything that we can master.*

MS: Yes. I think that three important features of our moral landscape would be transformed if we really did come to think of ourselves as, and were, wholly self-made men and women. We would lose a certain capacity for humility and restraint, not only with respect to our own natural talents but especially with respect to our children. It's an important fact about children that they are not wholly the product of their parents' will or the instrument of their ambitions. So humility is very much at stake here.

Also there would be an explosion of responsibility if people were held responsible for everything about them. It's morally redeeming and morally important that we aren't morally responsible for everything about us, and for that matter for everything that our children are or will become.

Finally, the moral basis of solidarity would be eroded if we came to think of ourselves as wholly self-made and wholly self-sufficient.

NW: *What then would you say to a child who, knowing you had sufficient funds and there was available technology, said: 'Dad I really, really wanted to be good at sport and you're the only one who wouldn't give me that and you could have done it'?*

MS: I would say: 'Go out and practise a bit longer.'

NW: *And the child would say: 'Practice isn't going to get me beyond all these genetically enhanced school colleagues I've got. I'm always going to be last in the race and that's your responsibility.'*

MS: Well, I would invite my child to ask himself or herself whether those genetically re-mastered or souped-up schoolmates weren't missing an important part of the purpose of sports, and maybe even the joy of the competition. I'd point out that some of the joy and some of the pride of success would be diminished if it were the product of a pill or tweaking of the genes.

NW: *In sport this is a losing battle, because sportspeople all over the world are already using every enhancement they can possibly find. Do you think the world is worse for that?*

MS: I think the world is and will be the worse insofar as the cumulative effect of technological enhancement and genetic enhancement will be a slide from sport to spectacle. Some people suggest that we should let the two exist side-by-side: have races where there are no holds barred, where all technologies are permitted, souped-up athletes, and so on; and have a second race for free-range slowpokes, and see which commands a greater audience. That's the challenge that's made by defenders of enhancement.

I think that in the short-run people might flood to the spectacle to see the robotic athletes. However, in time the audience would wane because spectacle exerts a certain allure, but only for a time; because it swamps or diminishes and erodes the human element, the nuance, the subtlety, the complexity of human beings negotiating with the limits of their own capacities. So I think the ratings would rise for a time, but then fade.

5

ALEXANDER NEHAMAS ON
Friendship

David Edmonds: *What special duties and obligations do we have towards our friends that we don't have towards strangers? Friendship plays a central part in most people's lives, and Alexander Nehamas, a distinguished professor of philosophy at Princeton, argues that it's a subject deserving of close philosophical scrutiny.*

Nigel Warburton: *We're going to talk about friendship. How did you become interested in the topic?*

Alexander Nehamas: Friendship is an extraordinarily important relationship in almost everybody's life, but, strangely enough, modern and contemporary philosophy have not paid much attention to it. So I thought that it was worth thinking about it in some detail—to see what contributions it makes to life and whether we can explain its significance in the life of most, if not all, of us.

NW: *Why do you think it has been neglected as a topic of discussion for philosophers?*

AN: Well, I think that a major reason is the following. Since the Enlightenment, and particularly in the last seventy-five years or so, we have had a tendency to identify all values with moral values. By moral values I mean values that enjoin us to treat everybody equally, to give the same respect and the same consideration to everyone in the world, independently of their status, race, gender, class, and everything else of that sort. Now, what is essential to friendship is *precisely* that you don't treat everybody equally; you give preference to your friends—you treat your friends better than you treat other people, you have more duties and obligations to them. And if you think that all value is moral and that to be a good friend is to neglect moral value, the best thing you can do may well be to neglect friendship as a subject of philosophical interest instead. Otherwise you may have to end up thinking that friendship is immoral and therefore a bad thing—something which obviously it is not. At least, that way you avoid confronting that dilemma.

NW: *Are you suggesting, then, that friendship is neutral from a moral point of view?*

AN: In the end, I hope to be able to say that friendship is profoundly valuable without locating its value in morality. In fact, it is not just valuable, but absolutely necessary to us—it is difficult to live without it. But its value is not the value attaching to moral behaviour. A whole other set of values, to which philosophy has paid no attention, is involved in friendship, values which I believe are also central to the arts. To put it very bluntly, and very roughly, the values of morality are values that depend on our commonalities: the similarities we already share and the similarities we hope to create among us. The values of friendship and the arts are exactly the opposite: they are values that depend on our differences from one another, on everything that makes one a distinct and interesting individual, someone with a particular and recognizable character or style. I believe that both kinds of value, the values of commonality and the values of individuality, are absolutely crucial in life. But I worry that we have paid too much attention to the values of commonality and I think that it is time to bring the other sort into view again.

NW: *I think it is important, then, to distinguish your use of 'friend' from a more common one, where it just means acquaintance.*

AN: The word 'friend' is very general. We can have very casual friends, very close lifelong friends, and everything in between. Of course, our most casual friends, who are no more than acquaintances, play a very limited role in our lives. Close friends, though, are absolutely essential to the development of our character and personality, and the role of people in between is, unsurprisingly, in between. But when you put all these relationships together, their effect, ideally, is to help constitute a person that is not only distinctive, but interestingly so. That 'interestingly', though, is unfortunately where the difficulties are.

NW: *That seems to put a lot of who we are outside our individual control. We can't choose completely the people we meet; and to some extent we can't even choose who our friends are, because we need them to like us as well as us liking them.*

AN: It is often said that friendship is a purely free and voluntary relationship. But of course it is not; it depends on all sorts of accidents and contingencies. Every one of us is to a great extent the product of factors over which we have no control. To take my own case, for example, I had no control over being born in Greece, over who my parents were, over the school they sent me to, over the fact that the school assigned me to a particular dormitory, which in turn limited the range of people who would become my friends, and so on. But for me freedom is less the ability to have chosen differently (which philosophers as different as Plotinus and Nietzsche actually take to reveal the very absence of freedom) than the willingness to recognize myself in what I have done, the ability to say: 'That was *my* action.' Accordingly, freedom is not indicated so much by the fact that I *chose* to do what I did but by the fact that it was *I* who chose it, of my own initiative and not because of some external factor. And that means that to regret my action is not to wish that I had chosen to act differently—for all I know, that is not possible—but to be disappointed in the sort of person my action shows me to be.

NW: So one of the values of friendship is the way in which our friends allow us to become who we wish to be.

AN: Our friends are even more important than that. They not only allow us, they orient us toward what we are to be and they are crucial to our becoming one kind of person rather than another. Whether the person we end up becoming is a person we wish to be or not is a separate question: friendship is by no means an unalloyed good.

NW: *People fall into friendships but they also fall out of them. Why do they fall out of friendship?*

AN: That can happen for many different reasons, but perhaps we could classify them, very roughly, into two kinds: either I have changed, or my friend has changed. At least that is the way we put it. My own sense is that to think that our friend has changed generally indicates that we ourselves have changed as well—except that our own changes are often invisible to us: we still seem to ourselves to be who we have always been. So a friendship, generally speaking, falls apart when the friends have gradually begun to take different directions in their lives and can no longer sustain the connection they had had up to that point. It can be very painful to 'fall out' of friendship, as you so well put it—no less painful than the end of a love affair.

The reason it is so painful is, I think, that when you can no longer be my friend you reveal, first, that you no longer like the person I am—which shows that the question 'What did I do wrong?' is always the wrong question to ask. For it is not what I *did* but, as we put it in everyday terms, *who I am*, that you no longer find attractive. Second, it reveals something that is even more painful—namely, that you no longer like the person *you* have become as a result of our friendship and that you want to give up something that I have been at least partly responsible for creating. And that shows that saying 'it's not you, it's me'—more common, to be sure, in love affairs but often said in friendships as well—is not a con-solation but a simple evasion, for you are responsible for the 'I' that is no longer satisfied with itself.

NW: *An aspect of that is the way that people change over time; friendship takes place over time, it is not just a relationship of the moment.*

AN: Taking place over time is absolutely crucial to friendship; it is also a main reason why friendship is more difficult to represent than we commonly think. It is close to impossible, for example, to recognize that a painting depicts two (or more) friends without a title to that effect or some similar literary artifice or allusion. The reason is that friends can be doing anything together and no single event is ever enough to indicate the presence of friendship. Sexuality and violence are relatively easy to represent because some of their visual marks are generally known. But friendship has no marks that are specific to it: even a painting of two people fighting could be a painting of friendship, since friends often fight with each other. Recognizing a friendship (even when it comes to realizing that *you* are or have become someone's friend) requires time—time to develop in the first place and time to flourish. As Aristotle says, you can't become someone's friend overnight. And I would add that you can't be someone's friend for a day.

NW: *Is that in part because to be a true friend to somebody involves understanding them and to understand somebody you have to see them in a range of situations?*

AN: Exactly. Where others see only a particular action on your part, your friend can see your whole personality expressed in it. And to be capable of that, friends have to have been exposed to a variety of each other's actions.

The parallel with the arts is handy here. What is it to recognize that a particular painting is by this painter rather than by anyone else? It is to recognize that painter's style, and to be capable of that you must have seen a large enough number of that painter's works. In the same way, you have to see a pattern in your friends' actions—a pattern that is only discernible with time. Seeing such a pattern is not so much the ability to predict what your friends will do as it is the ability to see what they do, once they have done it, as an expression of their character—and, in fact, it is often in their most *unpredictable* actions that their personality emerges most forcefully.

NW: *I can see the selfish value to me of having friends in that they help me to understand who I am. But what is the overall value of friendship?*

AN: If you are selfish you won't limit your friends' value to their contribution to your self-knowledge—you will also value them for being free with their money when you need it or with their getting you out of a difficult situation and so on. And our ability to rely on our friends is an important part of the value of friendship. But the good of friendship as a whole lies in its contribution to our becoming who we are and, in particular, to our becoming—if we do—arresting individuals. Friendship, the totality of our friends—among whom our close friends are the most important—is one of the main instruments or mechanisms that we employ in order to establish a path through life that is distinctly our own. Friendship, in other words, can't be accommodated within the constraints of morality because individuality is not always consonant with morality. Friendship and art have a distinct value of their own, dependent, as I said earlier, on individuation and differentiation rather than on similarity and solidarity with the rest of the world. But both are essential to life and sometimes, for better or worse, they come into conflict. And when they do, it is not clear to me that morality must always win. Philosophers have very often supposed—partly through the influence of Kant—that moral values should always prevail and—partly through a moralized reading of Aristotle's discussion of *philia*[1]—that they always do. But I am not sure they should.

NW: *Do you think that is because what we often value is the person, and one or two good actions are not what make a good person?*

AN: Well, people often get credit—and rightly so—for particular actions: you don't have to save lives more than once to be admired for your heroism, just as sometimes an author's reputation rests on a single novel and nothing else. In general, however, evaluation attaches primarily to the person and only secondarily to actions. For one thing, two actions can involve exactly the same kind of behaviour and yet express completely different character traits: the very same type of action can be in one context admirable and in another, contemptible. That is what Socrates was always insisting upon when he said, for example, that courage can't be defined as the willingness to stand your ground against the enemy, because standing your ground can

---

[1] The Greek word that Aristotle uses that is usually translated as 'friendship'.

sometimes be very foolish and, anyway, retreating in order to counter-attack can also be the brave thing to do in certain circumstances. It is not the behaviour that qualifies as courageous but the psychological trait, the character that is exhibited in it.

POLITICS

6

KWAME ANTHONY APPIAH ON
Cosmopolitanism

David Edmonds: *Kwame Anthony Appiah, of Princeton University, half-English, half-Ghanaian, a US resident, is the quintessential cosmopolitan. A cosmopolitan, by his definition, is someone who recognizes that people across societies have much in common, while also being tolerant of their differences. Negotiating these differences can be tricky—not least when what's at stake are deeply held moral or religious beliefs, such as those surrounding, in the oft-cited case, female circumcision or FGM (female genital mutilation). Appiah is optimistic that talking, discussing, conversing, engaging in respectful dialogue about difference, is the most effective way of resolving differences—or at least, the best way of learning to live with them.*

Nigel Warburton: *We are going to focus on cosmopolitanism. What do you understand by that term, 'cosmopolitanism'?*

Kwame Anthony Appiah: It is one of these words that got into English from the Greek. The Greek is *kosmopolites*, which means citizen of the cosmos, of the world; so it is really a way of talking about global citizenship. It is a particular tradition of talking about global citizenship that has two strands which are worth identifying. The first is the idea that we are all collectively responsible for one another: the idea that we are a sort of single moral community. But a lot of people think that, and they are not all cosmopolitans. What's distinctive about cosmopolitanism is the idea that, yes, we are all a moral community, but also that we are all entitled at the same time to live according to different modes of life. The cosmopolitans think it is good and interesting and fine that people live different modes of life; they don't want everybody to become the same, they don't want everybody to become Catholics, or Marxists or even perhaps liberal democrats.

NW: *So another of way of putting that, as you yourself have put it, is 'universalism plus difference'. And the 'universalism' is for some people hard to stomach: it isn't obvious that all human beings have a great deal in common beyond their biology.*

KAA: First of all it is important that we have a common biology because the base level of human well-being and human suffering comes from our shared biology. If you stick a pin into the arm of a Chinaman or a Yanomamö Indian neither of them will like it. The Yanomamö Indian will probably bash you over the head with a club, so there will be different responses, but the basic biological stuff is very important. You can take two possible views about this: one is a very practical view which is, 'let's just see what we agree about and start from there'. You can take a more philosophical starting-point and say, 'is there a basis for deciding that some views, whether or not they are held by the Chinese or the Yanomamö, are correct?', and then try to see what it would take to persuade everybody of the correctness of those views. At a certain level of abstraction, I think that the moral views of most of the people on the planet have quite a lot in common already. But this is at a certain level of abstraction, and it doesn't help in many cases where there are conflicts about what you ought to do. In those cases you are going to have to make arguments and see what can be done to persuade people of the correctness of your view. Now I don't think the cosmopolitan ought to be committed to any particular, elaborate philosophical view about the metaphysical status of morality, because that is exactly one of the controversial things that it would be difficult to drag into every conversation.

It would be better to start with a set of practices, talking and listening, and try to figure a way to work out what you can agree upon and what you can't agree upon. It is very important to recognize that that kind of conversational exchange, across quite wide cultural differences, can actually produce consensus about all sorts of very important things. Most people think it is bad when children die of diseases, for example; most people think we should do our best to cure them if we can. This is a very substantial kind of agreement. It is also important to notice that we live perfectly well in modern societies with neighbours with whom we disagree about some things. So the fact that there are these disagreements across the planet shouldn't make us think we can't live together in peace, any more than the fact that we have disagreements at home has made it impossible for us to live together in peace.

I live in the United States. It couldn't be more divided a
society on the question of abortion, but a surprisingly large
number of people, many of whom think that killing foetuses
is a very, very bad thing to do, are nevertheless willing to live
within a shared framework of law with people who don't
believe this.

NW: *Yes, indeed, and supporters and opponents of abortion agree on
many aspects of morality.*

KAA: Yes, very often when people disagree about what to
do it isn't a moral disagreement: it is just a disagreement
about how the world is, about what the facts are. If I thought
that there was a divine creator who had commanded us to
save foetuses, then, of course, I would go about the business
of saving foetuses. So some of these disagreements are just
disagreements about who, if anybody, runs the universe, and
what He or She wants. Other disagreements are just about
facts. Take female genital mutilation, a standard example of a
topic on which there is disagreement in the world. There
some of the background disagreements are about sexuality.
If you ask Dinka men why it is important to 'circumcise', as
they would put it, their women, they will say, 'because if we
don't, we will have to cope with an ungovernable sexuality'.
Now one thing you have then to show them is that in large
parts of the world uncircumcised women are perfectly able
to regulate their sexuality, and so probably this is a mistake.

NW: *In that particular case I can understand your approach leads to
greater empathy with the people who make those choices, even though
you disagree strongly with their choices. But I am not convinced that*

conversation will lead to a change in practice there. These are very ingrained beliefs that are resistant to rational debate.

KAA: Look, the claim isn't, and shouldn't be, that conversation will resolve everything. It won't. We have to learn to live with the fact that for the very long foreseeable future there will be disagreements within and across societies. And as the world becomes more and more like a single society, these will all be more like internal disagreements. But there will still be lots of disagreements. The conversation is aimed at being able to live with people, whether you agree with them or not. I have been giving lectures about the ways in which people actually change their minds about morality. On the whole they don't change their minds simply by being persuaded by some argument. Life changes in some way, or you get used to other people doing things, and then you think, 'Well why shouldn't we do that?' It is much less a matter of rational persuasion than perhaps a philosopher would like.

The practice of circumcising Kikuyu women in Kenya, for example, was on the way out after the Second World War and it only came back as a kind of counter-reaction to missionaries, and other people, saying how awful it was: people went into a nationalist mode, where they defended this practice as an expression of Kikuyu identity. So this is a case where, actually, if we had just left it alone it probably wouldn't be going on any more. There are important things to say to people about female genital mutilation, but they depend upon having had the conversation and figuring out what it is they think they are doing and why they are doing it. It is a very important fact in this debate that in many of the places where it is practised, the practice is thought of as a Muslim practice. And so it is equally important that there is nothing in the Koran about it. The practice is mostly carried out by people who don't read, and don't have their own access to the Koran. Simply telling them that there is a respectable Muslim traditional argument that says 'you mustn't do this' is informing them of something that they care about and that is relevant, given their beliefs as to whether they should do it.

NW: *This is a difficult case for a liberal, because you want to tolerate other people's practices. But if these practices are imposed on people who are not in a position to make an informed choice for themselves, children, for instance, you might want to be paternalistic and protect them from it for their own good. Adults making informed choices would be a different case.*

KAA: Paternalism is treating someone like a father, and children should be treated the way fathers should treat children. So, if we could stop female genital mutilation happening to children—if it was in our power—then, I think, of course, we should. The real question is what we can do to make it more likely it will stop. Look, if you send in the marines, it won't work. What happened in Kenya will be repeated: you'll turn it into a nationalist issue and it will probably raise the frequency with which it occurs. People who recognize that you take them seriously, that you want to understand their arguments, that you respect their right to be participants in a conversation, are more likely to see you as a reasonable interlocutor, or someone who might have a point. And so they are more likely to be persuaded. But in the end, change is going to happen because people in the societies where it is done will begin to agitate. Probably many of them will be women, and they'll refuse to have their own children treated in these ways. They'll learn from the fact that in the rest of the world people who don't do it seem to be doing okay, and that the bad things that they suspect might happen if they stopped aren't going to happen.

NW: *Let's look at a different problem that might arise for cosmopolitans. If you believe that fundamentally you are a citizen of the world, there may not be grounds for preferring the people nearest to you to those who might need your help who are very far away. There may be no reason to favour family and compatriots over those on the other side of the world who may be dying of poverty and malnutrition. Some philosophers have argued that what a responsible citizen of the world should do is treat all human needs equally, and that would involve us in the West giving most of our money to Oxfam or to UNICEF, one of the charities that might be able to save people's lives. Isn't that too demanding a morality?*

KAA: Part of what is important here is giving people a reasonable account of how they ought to conduct themselves. Addressing people in the richer parts of the world in the way that my friend and Princeton colleague Peter Singer does—by saying, basically, 'you ought to be depriving yourself of many, many of the things that are good in your life, because there are people out there who are suffering'— coming at people in that way, even supposing it were right, is not going to work. People are going to turn away from someone who makes what they will regard as absurdly demanding claims on them. So the first thing we have to think about is, what can we ask people to do that they might actually do, that would help with the problems in the world?

People who are engaged with the rest of the world, who know about life in places where people are poor and suffering—that is, people who have a cosmopolitan attitude and engagement with life—are more likely to be tractable, more likely to be persuadable to do something. Remember, though, I don't think that cosmopolitanism should come with heavy philosophical baggage, because then you are making it a condition of the conversation that people agree with you about something. The whole point about the conversation is that we will talk to whoever comes along. Still, my view is that we have the privilege of living in a world in which we have the resources to give everybody what they need in order to have the possibility of a decent human life, and the resources to do this without abandoning opera, and BBC Radio 3, and all those things that might seem optional if you were focused entirely on human suffering.

But, second, I think what we owe to others is less than many philosophical views claim. The reason is that many of these philosophical views are *maximizing* views: that is, they are views according to which we should make sure that everybody has the most of a possible thing. Whereas I think that what is crucial in moral life is to make sure that everybody has what they need in order to lead a decent life, which is not the same thing as everybody having the most we can get them, or even the same as everybody having an equal amount. The real point is that we have these baseline obligations. They are quite demanding; we are not meeting them, we should be doing more than we are. But they are not so demanding that your natural response is just to say, 'well, if that is what I am being asked to do, I might as well just block it out'. One of the extraordinary things about the present isn't actually the proportion of people who don't have a decent life—even though it is a very large number and we should be doing something about it—but it is the proportion of people who do.

NW: *That optimism runs through everything I have read of yours— and it is very inspiring to read. But post-9/11 most people have become depressed about what is possible in terms of world peace and learning to live with each other.*

KAA: About 9/11: I think people have wildly overreacted. Of course it was a terrible thing and the people who did it were wicked people. On the other hand, the number of people that they killed is very much smaller than the number of people that die on the American highways month by month, or year by year. And it turned out that you could inflict this massive attack on the centre of American business and the economy shrugged it off after a little while. There was a little hiccup. So it wasn't such a big deal, and the fact is, if they were so powerful they would have done things like that since, and often; and they haven't. They haven't because they haven't been able to. They would be even less able if we had better relations with, and understanding of, the Muslim world, in which they are, of course, exceptional extremists, but which nevertheless is a place within which they can, to some extent, hide from us. Many of the people who hide them don't approve of what they are doing and wouldn't do it themselves, but they are not going to hand them over to us either, because they don't think of us as their friends. And if we fail to distinguish between the extremists—who are murderous people whom we should try to capture and punish—and the rest, we will continue to have that problem.

So we have to have the intellectual clarity and the moral courage to go on relating to the Muslim world. The first thing we need to do in thinking about the Muslim world is to recognize that it is, as our world is—whatever we think of as *our world*, the West, Britain, some people think Christendom—internally, incredibly diverse. The traditional Muslim world runs from Morocco to Indonesia. Hundreds and hundreds of languages are spoken in the Muslim world. There are places in the Muslim world where women wear burkhas and places where they don't. These are all Muslim societies and they are very, very different. There are people in the Muslim world whom it is easy to talk to, who are delighted to share with us, for example as philosophers, the fact that their great Arab and Persian Muslim philosophers drew on the same roots as we did. They were students of Plato and Aristotle and so on; in fact, if they hadn't sustained those texts and looked after them during what we call our Dark Ages, we wouldn't have most of them, we wouldn't have Aristotle and Plato. So there are lots of people it is easy to talk to. We have to be willing to build the conversations with the very many people who would love to talk to us and we have to figure out a way of communicating with them. Of course we can disagree with them about lots of things, as they disagree with us and each other, but we respect what we share, our humanity and our right to a dignified life.

At the moment they don't believe we respect them. And the reason they don't believe it is because many of us don't respect them. They see that we don't treat them respectfully.

The United States, in its foreign policy (under President Bush), simply doesn't put the same weight on the views of people in the Muslim world as it does on the views of, say, people in Europe. This can't be denied—it is just a fact, and we ought to be trying to communicate and practise respect.

NW: *Much of our identity in life comes from our links to a particular place, to particular families. Doesn't that conflict with the cosmopolitan idea of being a citizen of the world?*

KAA: That is the point where the cosmopolitan's 'universality plus difference' really pays off. I said that we have these baseline obligations to everybody which we aren't meeting and we should be. But beyond that we are free to be partial. Any sensible moral view has to have a place for the idea that we are entitled—not just that we will, but that we are *entitled*—to care more about those whom we love in our families and those in our community with whom we share our practices, and those in our nation with whom we share together the responsibilities of running the state, and so on. We are entitled to be like that, just as we are entitled to place a greater weight on our own survival than the survival of other random people.

7

MIRANDA FRICKER ON
Credibility and Discrimination

David Edmonds: *Suppose, in a court case, members of a jury are more sceptical of black witnesses than white ones. Suppose a woman makes a point in a business meeting, and is ignored, while the same point, made by her male colleague, is greeted with nods and murmurs of approval. Miranda Fricker, a philosopher at Birkbeck, University of London, believes there's an important type of injustice going on here—an injustice that has hitherto been ignored. She labels it 'testimonial injustice'—and it's a type of injustice wrapped up with the theory of knowledge, what philosophers call epistemology. Testimonial injustice involves a hearer, or listener, not taking the statements of a speaker—a knower—as seriously as they deserve to be taken. If we're guilty of this we're guilty of not according the speaker appropriate respect.*

Nigel Warburton: *Knowledge and justice are two concepts philosophers tend to discuss independently of each other, but in your work you've brought them together. Could you say a little about how you did that?*

Miranda Fricker: Yes, for years I was interested in how issues of social identity and power impinge on how we operate as knowers and enquirers. And it's been something that's been talked about a lot in feminist philosophy but very rarely, if ever, in mainstream epistemology or ethics. My first interest has really been in the primary case of what I call epistemic injustice, namely testimonial injustice. That's when one person is telling another person something and the hearer, owing to some prejudice, deflates the level of credibility they give to the speaker. When that happens I think the hearer is doing the speaker a distinctive kind of injustice. She's undermining him specifically in his capacity as a giver of knowledge. So imagine, for instance, a white police officer pulling over a black driver to ask him 'Is this your car?' And the driver replies that it is. If the credibility afforded the driver by the police officer is deflated by racial prejudice, then the police officer has done the driver an injustice in his capacity as knower. More particularly, the speaker has been undermined in his capacity as a giver of knowledge. That seems to me a distinctive kind of epistemic injustice, which merits having its own label—testimonial injustice.

NW: *So the policeman who's got a prejudice doesn't give credibility to somebody from a particular ethnic group. Isn't that just an empirical question, a question about how people happen to behave?*

MF: In part it's certainly an empirical question, though I don't know of any sociology of knowledge which is specifically about this issue. There's a lot of sociology and social psychology about prejudice and stereotyping and there's very interesting work done in the United States by Claude Steele, for instance, about what he calls 'stereotype threat'.

For example, in one experiment using American students where the group is a mix of African-American and white American, if you tell them all that it's specifically an experiment to test intellectual ability, the black American students tend to do worse; whereas if you tell them specifically that it's not a test of intellectual ability, they don't do worse. The conclusion is that the imaginative presence of a negative stereotype of oneself as a member of a group who achieves less well intellectually than others is enough to cause you to perform less well. And there's a lot of that sort of empirical work that's fascinating and feeds into my interest in epistemic injustice. But I haven't yet discovered anyone who's looked at the particular mechanism of how prejudice affects levels of credibility given.

Now, something else you're raising in your question is how recognizable are these issues as genuinely *philosophical*? In the past many philosophers would have thought this just a matter of sociology of knowledge—a purely empirical matter. One is, after all, concerned with real-life phenomena, like who gets believed and who doesn't, or whose word is taken seriously. They'd have thought these are ethically important matters but they're not really philosophical questions, certainly not ones relevant to epistemology. But these days I don't think many people think like that in philosophy. And the theory of knowledge, specifically, has moved in the direction of taking ethical matters seriously. So there are lots of people doing what's called virtue epistemology, thinking about what sorts of virtues are needed on the part of knowers and enquirers (hearers, for instance—people who are, or should be, listening for the truth, attempting to listen beyond prejudices in order to pick up knowledge that's offered to them by no matter who). The surge in virtue epistemology has opened the door to seeing questions of epistemic injustice as genuinely philosophical, indeed genuinely epistemological, in a way that didn't used to be the case.

NW: *So it's injustice if you treat people unfairly. But some people are better sources of information than others. I would attribute greater authority to somebody who's trained for ten years as a doctor than to somebody who's just intuited what my illness would be.*

MF: That's exactly right. And that's why there's no testimonial injustice unless there's a prejudice there. So supposing it's the case that women know less about football than men. Now I might personally be a keen football fan, so that I'm unexpectedly expert on the relative talents of the players and on which teams are in what division, and yet somebody might be casting around for information about the recent score and not think to ask me because I'm a woman. Or I might express an opinion about one team and their first thought might be: 'What does she know about it?' Now I'm open to the possibility that they would be operating with an empirically reliable stereotype. So far as I know, women in general aren't great football enthusiasts; so other things being equal, it's relatively unlikely that a woman will know the recent football results, and so someone might reasonably overlook me as a potential informant and choose to ask a man instead. That's probably fair enough; I don't think such a person would have done me any injustice. Suppose, however, I start offering him evidence that goes against this reliable stereotype he's been using—maybe I start chatting in

an unusually well-informed way about this or that team—
and suppose he still doesn't hear me. That's the point where
his hanging on to the normally reliable stereotype comes to
be actually prejudiced. Because my behaviour is effectively
offering him lots more evidence (about me as a potential
informant about the score) to which he's blind. He's resisting
the new evidence because of the power of the stereotype
that's operating in his mind. But it's only at that point, in my
view, that prejudice is entering into it and that he's starting to
do me some sort of epistemic injustice.

NW: *Would you say it's an injustice to give somebody too much
credibility? For example, if Prince Charles starts pontificating about the
environment or architecture there's a kind of injustice done to him in
treating him as an expert in a field in which he might not be particularly
well educated.*

MF: That's another great question. I changed my mind
about this issue. When I first wrote about epistemic injustice
I talked as if not only 'credibility deficit' but also 'credibility
excess' was a case of epistemic injustice. But over time I came
to the view that credibility excess is not an epistemic
injustice, at least not in my sense. I think our intuition that
there is something very wrong with giving excess credibility
to, say, father figures is sound; but what's wrong with it is
we're assuming (probably quite often rightly) that such
a positive bias goes with some correlative negative bias:
too much credibility for father figures implies not
enough credibility for other figures. But my particular
concern is whether the individual speaker is wronged by
getting the excess level of credibility. And it seems to me

that if I give a paternal figure a credibility excess I don't thereby wrong *him*. So, although if you look at a system where one group is getting too much credibility there's bound to be another who's suffering a deficit, still the one who receives the excess is not thereby wronged.

NW: *I wasn't clear why the injustice that you talk about actually is an injustice. Is it because people lose their dignity through not being treated with respect, or is it because knowledge won't come out this way?*

MF: The injustice is the first thing—a matter of intrinsic insult. There is also the epistemic dysfunction which is the second thing you mentioned—the prejudiced hearer will tend to miss out on knowledge offered by certain sorts of speaker. Indeed, it's not just epistemically disadvantageous for him individually (he misses out on knowledge), it's also bad for the epistemic community as a whole. It's bad for all the enquirers and knowers who want the flow of information and ideas to be free of blockages. Where there's testimonial injustice there'll be less truth flowing, fewer good ideas flowing. But that's not where the injustice lies. The injustice lies in the way in which I undermine you as an individual, and specifically in your capacity as a knower, if I allow prejudice to deflate my credibility judgement of your word. To be recognized as a knower is to be recognized as rational; and we're all used to the general idea in the history of philosophy that our rationality is what gives human beings their special dignity, their special value. So if I undermine you in your capacity as a knower, then I undermine you in a capacity that is essential for human value.

There can be grave cases, and trivial cases. Where it's a racial prejudice and it really matters, for example at the end of Harper Lee's *To Kill a Mockingbird*, where we find the defendant being charged with rape just because none of the white jurors believe the word of a 'negro', then the injustice matters deeply, and indeed in that case the consequences prove fatal. But even if I undermine you only a tiny bit, because my hearing you with a prejudiced ear is of no real consequence to you or anyone else, still I've given a little pinprick at your very humanity. In either sort of case, momentous or trivial, the speaker is being undermined in a capacity that's essential to human value. That insult is the intrinsic wrong at the core of any epistemic injustice.

NW: *Is it fair to describe you as an ethicist in what you're doing? Your main interest is in right and wrong, not actually in how we come to know things?*

MF: Certainly; indeed, fifteen or so years ago that would have been the only natural way to put it. But in the last decade or two epistemology has moved in the direction of ethics in the general sense that a lot of people are now interested in what's called value-driven epistemology. And a key commitment of value-driven epistemology is that we focus on what sorts of virtues enquirers need to have in order to be good knowers and effective enquirers. This brings the business of ethics and epistemology closer together in everybody's mind.

NW: *What do you mean by virtue there? Is virtue just a habit?*

MF: Habit is certainly the crux of the matter. Let me give the relevant example of virtue. The particular virtue that the hearer needs to have, in order to counteract the ever-present risk that he or she is going to allow a prejudice to deflate the credibility she gives to a given speaker, is some sort of corrective virtue. Let's assume—this is my own pessimistic view—that prejudices often enter into our judgements without our permission, so that even if I'm a thoroughly unprejudiced person at the level of my beliefs, still my judgements of credibility might be affected by prejudice. Let's say I'm a card-carrying feminist and all my beliefs are in very good order sexism-wise, and I don't believe for a moment that women politicians don't have good enough judgement or statesmanlike *gravitas* to be world leaders; still, it seems to me, our collective social imagination is full of prejudiced stereotypes of political authority that give men a significant advantage—witness the notion of 'statesmanlike' behaviour and so forth. Now for all I know, when a woman politician is up there on the platform asking for my vote, somehow I just don't take her word quite as seriously as the similarly skilled male politician next to her. If so, I need to have some kind of corrective mechanism to try and make sure that doesn't happen, or not for long. Some kind of mechanism that prompts me to ask myself, how should I really compare these two speakers? And if I am able to make that corrective mechanism habitual, then it seems to me I'm on my way to possessing a distinctive intellectual-ethical virtue.

NW: *From a practical point of view, if I take seriously your theory, how am I going to change my behaviour?*

MF: Well I don't know—you may be thoroughly virtuous! For my part I think if prejudice is entering in at the level of *belief*, rather than more stealthily by way of stereotypical images, then we'll have some ability to police our own judgements, so that we can adjust our beliefs in the appropriate way. But the trouble may be significantly worse even if our beliefs are in okay shape. Let's say we're still living in a relatively socially immobile class-driven society, and let's say you have no class-prejudiced beliefs. Nonetheless, you may have reason to fear that prejudiced attitudes and ideas subtly influence your judgements—so what should you do about it? One of the great problems here is that there's a lot of empirical evidence to suggest that in policing one's own prejudices by paying lots of negative attention to those prejudices only makes it worse. So ideally what we ought to do is just try and change our habits without too much reflection, find some way of practising giving higher levels of credibility to the groups you fear you may be giving too low levels to. That's what some equal-opportunities training programmes aim to help us do. What one hopes to achieve is a change to one's spontaneous, unreflective habits of social perception and credibility attribution.

On the other hand, there's a place for reflection and critical awareness. Like most ethical phenomena, once you become more aware of testimonial injustice (whether you're on the delivering or receiving end, or both), so that you can recognize it and put a name to it when it happens, then you're surely in a better position to do something about it. If you're on the receiving end, then you can make a complaint, you can protest it; if you're dishing it out, you can admit it and maybe make amends. I don't expect people to start using the words 'testimonial injustice', but the notion of *credibility deficit* might be a useful label—something to help bring out this implicit aspect of unequal opportunities. We're all aware of occasions where people suffer credibility deficit in the workplace—round the meeting-room table, or whatever it may be, somehow nobody quite hears her point until the other guy makes it in his voice. The driving prejudice on any given occasion may be to do with gender, or with race, or it may be to do with class, or accent, or whatever it is, but it's useful to have a label like 'credibility deficit' to help inform our understanding of the sometimes very subtle ways in which people can be unjustly undermined by epistemic discrimination.

8

ANNE PHILLIPS ON
Multiculturalism

David Edmonds: *The phenomenon of mass migration has made the tension between liberalism and multiculturalism one of the most hotly debated topics in contemporary political theory. Multiculturalists believe that members of minority groups should have the right to lead their lives as they see fit. But what happens when certain minority values clash with the values of the majority? Professor Anne Phillips is at the London School of Economics and is the author of several books on liberalism, multiculturalism, and feminism.*

Nigel Warburton: *The topic we want to talk about is multiculturalism. What do you understand by the term?*

Anne Phillips: Well, I think of it as having three components. First of all it involves saying that people's cultural identity matters to them: so ignoring or disparaging cultural identity is a harm. Second, the implication is that if you're in a society that contains a diversity of cultures, typically through histories of migration, then it's not appropriate to expect everyone to adopt the values, practices, and traditions of the dominant majority group. And, third, the public-policy implication is that it's likely that the laws and institutions will reflect the values and practices of the dominant or majority group; so this is a bias that needs to be either justified or undone.

NW: *That view can clearly come into conflict with a liberal attitude which encourages people to focus on their freedoms. Because at a certain point people's freedoms impinge on one another.*

AP: It's important to recognize that multiculturalism, in a sense, derives from liberal principles. It derives from principles of *equality*: ensuring that majority and minority groups are treated equably and fairly. It derives from principles of *freedom*: if I have the freedom to live my life according to my own values and beliefs, then why don't you? And it derives from the liberal principle of *toleration*: respecting even those differences you find challenging or demanding. However, having said that, there are obvious areas of conflict. If respecting cultural difference means, for example, respecting the rights of people who have very different ways of treating their children, like the extensive use of corporal punishment, or who have different values about the roles of women and men that might involve very constraining and oppressive conditions for women, then that clearly throws up potential problems.

NW: *Well let's take that example with the role of women. Suppose you were dealing with a culture where education for women was actually frowned upon. Liberalism would clearly come into conflict there with a multiculturalism that respects every culture's view of the good life. A liberal would want to give opportunities to everybody within a particular society.*

AP: Yes, I think there are real conflicts there. But part of the conflict comes about because of the particular notion of culture we're operating with. This is a notion that has endorsed the view that cultures can be represented by the spokes*men* of a particular cultural group, usually men, usually older, who explain what are the cherished practices and values of their group, often in ways that are completely at odds with what others in that group might say are their cherished practices and values. In the literature this is often talked of as the minorities-within-minorities problem. You want to set in train policies that ensure that minorities within society are not treated unfairly or disadvantaged, but some of the mechanisms you put in place may have the effect of removing protections from minorities *within* minorities, typically children, women, homosexuals, groups who are marginalized within the minority. But a lot of the problem here derives from an interpretation of multiculturalism which has taken culture in this very bounded sense of a cultural group whose needs, interests, and desires can be interpreted just through its spokesmen—a group that is thought to have a unified experience and voice. We need a multiculturalism that dispenses with that particular understanding of culture.

NW: *I'm not sure how that would work in terms of homosexuality in relation to Islam, for instance. Is there the scope for what I would see as the liberal approach to homosexuality within an Islamic subculture in, say, Britain?*

AP: Well, there are Muslim gays and lesbians, so at one level the answer is clearly 'yes'. I have also heard liberal Muslims talk about it being a principle of Islam that one doesn't interfere with one's neighbour's practices, and deriving from this an argument which didn't necessarily endorse homosexuality, but certainly sounded quite like the classically liberal notion that it's not for me to judge or criticize what you do in private. This is obviously a very heated issue. One of my worries about some of the current discourses about multiculturalism—I mean here, discourses that attack multiculturalism—is that they could encourage communities that feel themselves under threat to close in on themselves, and start defining their core traditions in much more restrictive ways. Where this happens the scope for opening up the possibility of being a Muslim gay may get closed down.

NW: *You're suggesting that our conception of a Turkish culture or an African culture is too crude if it's being created by the dominant group within that culture. So what's the alternative? How do we achieve an adequate definition of a particular culture?*

AP: One distinction people sometimes make—which I quite like though I don't consistently operate with it—is that we should stop using the noun 'culture', which always conjures up this sense of something very unified, very bounded. But we can't give up on the adjective 'cultural', for we are all enormously shaped by cultural influences and cultural norms. I don't know if you ever saw the film *The Magdalene Sisters*? It's based in Ireland in the 1950s and '60s, when the Magdalene laundries existed as places where families would send their daughters who had in some way offended against social and sexual norms. They had become pregnant outside marriage or maybe behaved in ways which were regarded as

sluttish or sexually loose. And the fathers, in consultation
with the local priest, would in effect incarcerate their
daughters in these laundries. Nowadays in Ireland this would
be regarded as an unbelievably cruel practice. Clearly you
have to use the notion of culture or cultural shift to explain
this. The 1950s and '60s was a period characterized by very
strongly held views about sex outside marriage being a sin,
when the Catholic Church still had enormous authority and
fathers still had enormous authority over their children.
There has been what we would regard as a cultural shift. But
having said that, it was never the case that all fathers locked
up their pregnant daughters in Magdalene laundries. Some
families were more horrified than others; some were
horrified but nonetheless supported their daughters; and
some (though probably not many in Ireland in the 1950s) were
relatively untroubled by the transgression. So we need to
have an understanding of cultural influences that allows us
to recognize the enormous diversity within what we as a
form of shorthand describe as 'culture'. It's quite a dangerous
shorthand. Talking about 'Irish culture' or 'Turkish culture'
or 'African culture' is a risky and implausible shorthand.

NW: *Now, within a culture, assuming we can adequately define one,
it's still possible that, for instance, a woman would completely go along
with what you might see as an oppressive practice because of what a
Marxist would call a 'false consciousness'. She didn't really understand
what she needed to make her life go well, and just bought into what you
or I might see as a culturally oppressive regime.*

AP: This is a very real and important point. One qualifica-
tion I would make before answering is that I don't think the

general idea of the happy slave is very plausible. Mostly I think it's a figment of the philosopher's imagination. When there is oppression, people tend to notice it. Having said that, of course you're right: there are situations in which some-body else is living a life which I might consider deeply oppressive and she says to me, this is my choice: this is what I want to do. What then? My view is that in the end you have to listen to what people say. Of course there are all kinds of social policies to ensure people really do have alternatives: these would include housing provision, educational policies, legal services, all the kind of things which make it more real for people to say: 'Yes, I can see the alternatives and this is my choice.' And of course, talking is great; we all change our ideas about what's possible through talking. But if at the end of it somebody says, 'You may think this is oppressive but this is my choice', I just think we have to listen to people.

NW: *That makes complete sense with reasonably well-informed adults. But many of the choices we talk about—female circumcision, some arranged marriages—occur when people aren't adults and when they're not reasonably well-informed.*

AP: I have to say I think this is one of the most difficult areas. With children, there is no question. Public authorities have the responsibility to protect children. I don't endorse in any way female genital cutting or other harms to young children. The difficult area is young people between the ages of 12 and 18: at what point do you say, 'This is your decision', and at what point do you say that you are so much at the mercy of the influences and pressures of your family and community that we need to step in and protect you? But this is the kind of problem that the law is dealing with all the time, it is not something specific to particular kinds of cultural group. When is someone a child and when an adult? That's a very difficult issue, and I don't feel I have secure answers. I'm very clear that with adults you listen to what they say and I'm very clear that with children you protect them. But of course a lot of difficult issues come in the middle.

NW: *I suppose with reversible decisions it's not the end of the world if people make a decision that's bad for them and can later undo it. But some things aren't reversible.*

AP: That's one criterion some people have suggested: that you should ban any kind of irreversible decision.

NW: *If you're trying to assess whether somebody freely chose something, their choice to remain within that community could be an index. So one test might be whether somebody chooses to remain within a community. Is that a fair point?*

AP: It's only a fair point against the background of a genuine range of alternatives. Simply interpreting people's decisions to stay as evidence that they actively endorse the life that they're living can be a very mean-minded way of reading what people are doing, unless you have a secure basis for saying that they really do have alternatives. For example, that there are jobs they could take, places they could live, that there are support networks for them, that they could have a genuinely alternative life.

NW: *If we had an analogous case where a woman chose to stay with a husband who beat her, we'd say that her choice to stay there is not* *really an indication that she wants that kind of life. It just might be that she can't see a way out.*

AP: That's right. We would regard it as a rather cruel reading—at least I hope we would—to say: 'Well, she's staying with him, it's her choice, so we can't see a problem with the fact that he continues to beat her.' We do think it's a problem that he continues to beat her. But mostly we understand why it is that people are very reluctant to give up on relationships. They hope that there's a chance that he may change. Of course, sometimes, sadly, they're wrong, and to read their decision to stay as evidence that there's no problem is misleading. But the complete opposite to that, saying this woman doesn't know what she's doing, is also problematic.

NW: *What about a classic problem of multiculturalism in Britain? There was a case recently of a primary-school teacher who wanted to wear a full veil for religious reasons and it was felt by a number of people that this was inappropriate because it was impossible for children to see her mouth when she was speaking—there were detrimental effects from an educational point of view. There's a conflict between a culturally or religiously motivated style of dress and the practical difficulties of using that kind of dress as a teacher. Do you have a way of resolving that kind of difficulty for multiculturalism?*

AP: To the extent that I have a formula, my formula is very basic. I'm against things which cause physical and mental harm and I'm against things which treat people unequally—which includes practices that treat women as inferiors to men. The difficulty in any culturally diverse society is how you interpret 'harm' and how you interpret 'equality'. In the case of the *niqab*, the full face veil, there are good practical reasons, to do with the needs of communication between teachers and students, why it's not appropriate in the classroom. In the case you're talking about, the teaching assistant was happy to reveal her face in the classroom but wanted to cover her face when there were male teachers present. Well, I also think that it's a bit problematic sending a message to 11-year-old children that it's impossible for men and women to engage in face-to-face communication. So for both those reasons I think her wearing the *niqab* in the school was problematic. But I also think it's very important that the decision about such cases isn't made on the basis that that woman, though she doesn't know it herself, is oppressed. The woman has made her choice, and she's made it on the basis of her interpretation of religious requirements.

NW: *So would it be fair to say that you still see multiculturalism as the best way to organize a society that contains many different groups?*

AP: If you set up multiculturalism as opposed to monoculturalism, multiculturalism has to be the way forward. Because monoculturalism is inequitable, it's oppressive, it's coercive. But I would argue for what I rather polemically call a multiculturalism without culture; a multiculturalism no longer premised on the solidified notions of culture that encourage and promote cultural stereotypes, and prevent us developing the kind of multicultural diversity I support.

9

WILL KYMLICKA ON
Minority Rights

David Edmonds: *The idea that individuals should have rights is now deeply embedded in western liberal democratic culture. But the idea that groups—such as, say, immigrants, Muslims, Jews or Sikhs, native Americans or French-speaking Canadians—the idea that they should have special rights seems incompatible with the kind of equality that liberals advocate. Nonetheless, Canadian philosopher Will Kymlicka believes that liberalism and group rights are compatible—in fact, not just compatible but in certain cases, he says, liberalism actually requires granting distinctive rights to groups.*

Nigel Warburton: *The topic we want to discuss is minority rights. The obvious questions to ask are: 'What is a minority?' and 'What kind of rights are we talking about?'*

Will Kymlicka: In my work I've generally focused on three different types of groups. First of all indigenous people; I'm from Canada so it's a very important issue for us. Secondly, historical, regional, linguistic minorities like the Quebecois or the Catalans or the Flemish. Thirdly, immigrant groups. Each of these groups has valid claims for certain kinds of rights against the state, but they're quite different and we need to look at them separately.

NW: *So you're saying these kinds of groups have special rights distinct from ordinary citizens' rights?*

WK: Yes. I think all liberal democracies have to respect a basic catalogue of civil and political rights. But a multicultural liberal democracy goes beyond that to recognize certain group-specific rights that are intended to remedy the particular types of injustices that these different groups often suffer from.

NW: *I can see there's going to be an immediate problem: how do you identify which groups are eligible for this treatment?*

WK: There are hard cases and easy cases. Before we get to the hard cases, we should recognize that there are certain distinct patterns. For example, indigenous people in the New World settler states—Canada, Australia, United States, New Zealand—share a lot in common. They face fundamentally different challenges from those facing recent immigrants or regional minorities. This threefold typology of groups is actually more effective than you might think—most minorities in the West do fall under one of these familiar types. Of course, there are some hard cases. For example, the Roma in continental Europe do not fit into any of these three categories. But even here it helps us understand what's distinctive about the Roma case to figure out how the Roma differ from these three patterns.

NW: *So we've got the three patterns—what do you want to say about what rights each group has?*

WK: As I say, my idea is that we think about rights as remedies for predictable types of injustices. So the first question is: what's the nature of the relationship between the state and these groups? How have these groups come to be incorporated into the state, and what are the standard kinds of injustices that arise in that relationship?

The case of indigenous people is perhaps the clearest case—they were colonized. That's a gross injustice. They were pushed off their lands, they were denied the right to maintain their own language, their own legal and political institutions were suppressed. So, it's not difficult to see that there were predictable injustices in that historic colonial relationship, and to see how respecting land claims and self-government rights help to remedy that injustice.

Compare that with the very different case of immigrant groups. They're not necessarily the victims of historic injustice because they're relatively recent arrivals. But there are still issues about how they become incorporated into the state. Western democracies have rules in place which state that in order for immigrants to become citizens, and to be able to participate fully in society they have to go through a number of steps and tests. There are now citizenship tests in Britain, as in most western democracies. In these tests, immigrants are required to learn the national language, to learn something about the history and culture of society, and they're expected, or required, to participate in institutions that were set up by the historic community. I think many of these requirements are quite reasonable, but we have to ask, what are the ways in which immigrants are disadvantaged or stigmatized, perhaps unintentionally, by the expectations of the larger society? And I think there are many contexts in which multiculturalism policies for immigrant groups can overcome these injustices, and make it easier for them to participate more fully and equitably in society.

NW: *Do immigrants as a whole form one group or are there sub-sections of immigrant groups: Polish immigrants, Chinese immigrants, and so on?*

WK: There are some generic issues that apply to all immigrants. For example, wherever immigrants come from, the state has a duty to assist them in learning the national language. If you're going to require that immigrants learn the national language to become citizens, you have to enable and assist them to learn the national language. There are other kinds of claims that are much more distinctive to particular immigrant groups, and one of the most important is the issue of racism. White European ethnic groups in Britain or in Canada or Australia have an easier time than more recent racialized minorities, and different policies are needed to deal with racism. One of the interesting issues in multiculturalism in all of these countries is this: we have one set of policies that are primarily about the accommodation of cultural diversity, religious diversity, or linguistic diversity for immigrants; then we have another set of policies that are about fighting racism and discrimination. And I think both of those are equally important parts of a larger multiculturalism.

NW: *What are the special rights that we should accord to specific minorities in a liberal society?*

WK: I don't like the term 'special rights' because that immediately makes people think that they are privileges.

So in the case of indigenous people, as I said before, it's primarily in relation to land and self-government, but also rights with respect to the control of natural-resource development on their traditional territories. In the case of historic regional minorities, such as the Quebecois or Catalans, official language rights are an absolutely critical part of the accommodation of sub-state nationalism. In the case of immigrant groups, the most well-known and controversial examples concern exemptions from existing laws to accommodate distinctive beliefs, such as exempting Sikhs from motorcycle-helmet laws or dress codes or accommodating dietary requirements in schools and hospitals and so on.

NW: *But one consequence of this sort of treatment is surely the suspicion that they're getting preferential treatment?*

WK: That's the standard criticism. Much of my work has been devoted directly or indirectly to trying to answer that. Part of the answer is to remind people how much existing institutions are a massive system of preferential treatment for the majority. It's their language which is the official language; it's their history which is taught in schools; it's their religion that's accommodated in the public holidays; and so on. So much of what we're trying to do through multiculturalism policies is to accord the same level of respect and accommodation for minorities that majorities take for granted and that they achieve through the normal majoritarian processes.

NW: *I was thinking about New York, where there are many immigrants, and after a generation or two they're not necessarily recognizably part of an immigrant population, they're just New Yorkers.*

At what point does a new immigrant cease to be accorded the distinctive minority rights?

WK: Firstly, there's very strong evidence that the children and grandchildren of immigrant groups continue to have a strong attachment to their ethnic identity. Sociologically speaking, this attachment to their ethnic identity is quite thin or even symbolic. It doesn't determine what their jobs are going to be; it doesn't determine who they're going to marry; it doesn't determine where they'll live. But they still take pride in being a Greek-American or a Japanese-American. It's important that that sense of ethnic identification be honoured and respected, for example, through kinds of multicultural education. That's not something that goes away with the first generation. To respect people's ethnic identities is an enduring requirement in a multi-ethnic society.

Other kinds of multiculturalism are more transitional. Some policies are primarily for that first generation or the children of immigrants who, for example, may need special assistance for learning the national language. That's no longer a relevant issue for the second or third generation. Multiculturalism for immigrants has both these transitional elements and enduring elements.

NW: *Where do you set the limits of what rights you accord a minority group? I'm thinking, for instance, of the sort of groups which might come from a country where polygamy is tolerated, or where there are arranged marriages.*

WK: My conception of multiculturalism is an explicitly liberal one. I evaluate claims for minority rights on the basis of what I take to be the core liberal values of individual freedom: equality of opportunity or equality of life chances, and democratic citizenship and effective participation. So, obviously, many claims that groups might make do not enhance individual freedom or equality of life chances or democratic participation, in which case they're not compatible with the liberal democratic constitution and I'm not interested in defending them.

NW: *You've worked with the Canadian Government—can you say a little bit about what it was like being a philosopher advising politicians?*

WK: Well, I found it very encouraging. I was pleasantly surprised at the extent to which bureaucrats and policymakers are deeply concerned with the normative and conceptual nature of their work. In their day-to-day work they are incredibly busy, they don't have time to sit back and think. But they're aware of these deep, philosophical questions such as 'What does fairness require in a diverse society?' and 'What are the limits of toleration?' These are issues that they wish they had time to think about in a more principled or conceptual way, rather than as an ad hoc response to new surprises or crises. If a philosopher can come along and frame those issues in a way that makes sense to them, they're very interested—I haven't had people reacting with: 'Well, you're just an ivory-tower philosopher, what you're talking about is not relevant for what we're doing.'

NW: *Has it changed the way you do philosophy?*

WK: I'm very interested in the relationship between case studies and theories. From the start of my academic career

I have been frustrated with the way many of my colleagues operate. They think that the right way to do normative political theory on these issues is to sit in a rocking-chair somewhere and try to deduce from one's mind what a group is, what culture is, what identity is, and then what rights groups or cultures or identities have. I think it's much more helpful to take some actual examples of groups making claims, and figure out what exactly is the claim they're making and how specifically does it relate to values of freedom, democracy, equality, and so on. So, having interaction with a government has exposed me to a lot of interesting cases that I wouldn't have known about otherwise; and it has also reaffirmed my commitment to that way of proceeding.

When philosophers think about the question of cultural diversity, they almost immediately jump to the conclusion that the real issue, the heart of the issue, is cultural relativism: are there universal values or are our values culturally relative? That debate has been going on for 2,000 years and it will go on for another 2,000 years. But it doesn't actually help us grapple with what's distinctive about contemporary debates around multiculturalism. We're living in a specific historical moment—we can think of it as a post-civil-rights epoch, starting in the 1960s—defined by the emergence of new political movements and new political claims, which include ethnic minorities as well as women, gays, people with disabilities, and so on. I think the task of the political theorist is to figure out what's new and distinctive about these kinds of collective identity claims.

NW: *I'm intrigued by that. Could you give an example of one of these new claims?*

WK: What this issue has exposed is that liberal democracy for the last 200 years or so has been intimately linked to the nation state. That's a demonstrable, empirical, historical fact. But most liberal political philosophy has not acknowledged it. One of the interesting things about the multiculturalism debate is that it helped to highlight the extent to which liberalism has actually been predicated on or dependent on nationhood. This is not necessarily a problem in itself—on the contrary, the ability of liberal values to take root in society has often been enhanced by the fact that they're linked to ideas and ideologies and institutions of nationhood. On the other hand, this linkage has clear potential to be unjust to these different kinds of minorities who do not share the characteristics that are assumed to define the nation.

So we have an inherited practice of liberal democracy which is linked (even, I might say, addicted) to nationhood, and it's now being challenged by a series of minority groups, many of whom share those liberal democratic values but feel that they have been excluded or stigmatized or disadvantaged by the link between liberalism and nationhood. So, the task we face at this historical moment is to find either a new conception of nationhood, or a way of decoupling liberalism from nationhood. That has generated a fascinating debate which has very little to do with the perennial question of cultural relativism.

NW: *You've been talking about a liberal position. As I understand it, a classic liberal position focuses on individual rights, not group rights.*

WK: Any liberal theory must include firm protection of a basic catalogue of individual, civil and political rights.

That's absolutely true. But the question is whether that catalogue of universal individual rights can and should be supplemented with group-specific minority rights. I actually think that this perception that liberalism is only compatible with individual rights is an artefact of the Cold War. There's a story to be told about how liberals like Karl Popper and Isaiah Berlin redefined the liberal tradition so that its single most defining feature was this kind of individualism, so as to maximally distinguish it from 'collectivist' Communism. Actually the liberal tradition is much more capacious, historically, in combining individual and group rights, and we can learn from that history.

NW: *Here's a pessimistic comment: since 9/11, many people think multiculturalism is doomed as a project.*

WK: It's absolutely true that people's openness to the claims of minorities depends on a basic level of existential security. If people think that minorities are a threat to that existential security, the space for multiculturalism often disappears. But we need to be careful in jumping to conclusions about the relationship between multiculturalism, understood as this set of distinctive rights, and the threats of radicalism, say amongst Muslim youth. If you look across the western democracies, we have cases of 'home-grown terrorism'; this has emerged in countries that have multiculturalism policies like Britain and Canada, but also in countries that don't, like Spain or Germany. All of these countries have arrested groups who were planning various acts of violence. So multiculturalism clearly is not the cause of radicalism: the problem is found whether or not there are such policies.

The key question is whether we can use multiculturalism policies to help address that problem: are there ways in which multiculturalism can be used as a way of addressing the sources of anger or resentment or hatred? There's probably more we could do about that.

One of the standard criticisms of multiculturalism in Britain has been that it was traditionally focused almost exclusively on race as the organizing concept, to the neglect of the distinctive issues raised by religion, and particularly Islam. So an important challenge is whether we can find a form of multiculturalism that doesn't just deal with issues of racialization, but also is a form of multiculturalism in which Muslims can find a home.

10

WENDY BROWN ON
Tolerance

David Edmonds: *Who could possibly be against tolerance? Isn't tolerance the mark of a civilized society, the quality that allows individuals with widely different lifestyles and values to rub along together in peace? Isn't tolerance unquestionably a good thing? Wendy Brown, Professor of Political Science at UC Berkeley, wants us to be a little more sceptical about the concept—though she tolerated a cross-questioning from* Philosophy Bites.

Nigel Warburton: *The topic we are going to discuss is tolerance. You have chosen the word 'tolerance' rather than 'toleration'; could you just explain why you prefer it?*

Wendy Brown: When 'toleration' is used, it almost always refers unconsciously, if not consciously, to the Reformation and the regime of toleration that was inaugurated in response to the problems of Protestant sects, bloody religious wars, and the persecution of sectarians and dissidents. Today the word 'tolerance' is used in a much broader, wider way. I have set 'toleration' aside because it almost always calls up that particular historical formation and problematic, and because 'tolerance' is the word that almost everyone uses today to talk about the problem we're about to talk about.

NW: *What got you thinking about tolerance?*

WB: What really sparked my interest in the problem of tolerance was how widespread its use became in the 1990s. One might have imagined that the concern with tolerance as we have understood it over the last several hundred years could have more or less died out. That is to say, tolerance emerged in the West primarily as something concerned with religious belief, where there was one hegemonic religion and then a set of other beliefs that had to be dealt with in some way or another by that hegemonic religion. Instead of dying out, what you see in the 1990s is an enormous renaissance in the use of 'tolerance'; it is used to talk about everything from political regimes to ethnicities, to cultures, to sexualities. It is also used to talk about religious beliefs— but not primarily so.

NW: *Tolerance is perhaps the prime virtue of a liberal society, and most people will have a prejudice in favour of tolerance: it seems to be the basis of any kind of multiculturalism, of any thriving society which recognizes the diversity of people within it. How could you be against tolerance?*

WB: I am not *against* tolerance, but I do want to submit it to close scrutiny, to ask what the concept is actually doing. The commonplace view is that tolerance is an absolutely benign virtue. Every smart, sane, civilized, human being has to be for it. So I start there and I ask: 'Okay, so what is this benign virtue?' If you actually look closely at the etymology of tolerance, what do you see? Across every disciplinary field in which it is used, from mining, to minting, to engineering, to pharmaceutical research, to social life, tolerance is always about the management of some undesirable element or foreign body, invading or taking up residence within the host. It is about an element that one would rather not have to deal with—whether the 'one' is a scientist or a social theorist or a political actor. Tolerance is always about *managing* some object of aversion, which is different, and different with a stigma—different as a problem. The host is neutral. The host is normal. The host is regular. The tolerated object is always, in some ways, problematic.

For example, in my country, there's a great history, or mythology, of Northern tolerance towards blacks compared to Southern bigotry. Certainly such tolerance seems generally preferable to slavery, lynching, *de jure* segregation, and the like. But tolerance is not freedom, equality, or justice—rather, tolerance is what it sounds like, suffering someone's existence rather than dealing with them violently. Moreover, tolerance means permitting someone to exist within a certain set of conditions, a certain set of constraints, and a certain set of limits on behaviour. It is this that I wanted to explore: why we were getting so much talk about tolerance in the 1990s in the United States, in an increasingly multicultural Europe, and in worldwide civilizational discourse. Why was tolerance becoming the mantra at the United Nations, when, peered at closely, one realizes that that word is always being used to handle something or someone that is abject, subject or subordinated, and to do so in a very particular way.

NW: *We surely need some kind of tolerance just to live with other people, don't we?*

WB: Absolutely we need some, just to get along with our neighbours and our colleagues, sometimes even our children. We have to tolerate certain things; we have to tolerate music we don't like, cooking-smells we might prefer didn't exist, behaviours of certain people on public transportation, and so forth. We think the best thing to do, and I agree with this, is to handle these things without making a fuss. But that kind of tolerance is very different from what I am talking about. That is a kind of tolerance, at a personal level, that is unquestionably essential to just getting along in the world. What I am concerned about is when tolerance is raised to a political principle and used as a substitute for discourses of justice, equality, or even freedom. What I am suggesting is that when it is raised to the level of a political principle of that sort, it usually cloaks the kinds of powers that are at issue. It cloaks inequalities; it even sometimes substitutes for egalitarian projects.

NW: *Could you give an example just to clarify what you mean there?*

WB: Sure. I'll give you an example that comes out of the 2008 US elections. Some of your listeners/readers may be aware that on many of the state ballots there were propositions challenging the legality of gay marriage. All of these propositions succeeded. That is to say, in the four states in which they were on the ballot, in each case, gay marriage was rendered illegal—usually by declaring that marriage should be officially defined as a relationship between a man and a woman. Now, the reason for mentioning this is that what many people said in treating these propositions—and indeed what presidential contender John McCain and vice-presidential contender Sarah Palin said—is, 'we are not *for* gay marriage but we are for tolerance [of gay people]'. This is also exactly what George Bush had said during his period as president.

If you step back from this for a second, you realize that what they are saying is 'we are not for marriage equality, but we are for tolerance'. So, quite literally, what is being suggested is that certain people will be tolerated instead of made equal. And that is the way tolerance has operated for most of its history in the modern West: it is always a kind of substitute for equality, or supplement to equality. Now, again, that is not the worst possibility if the alternative is extinction or persecution or death or exclusion from basic rights. Again, I am not *against* tolerance, but I do think that our tendency to just get sleepy and happy when we hear the word 'tolerance' is a problem.

NW: *What you are doing, in a way, is drawing attention to a word, a word that has smuggled within it a kind of patronizing attitude to the people who are tolerated. That occurs not just within a state or within a country, but actually in terms of a country looking outwards at other people.*

WB: Correct. One of the things that happened during the course of my research on tolerance was the event that has come to be known as 9/11. Right after the attacks on the World Trade Centre and the Pentagon, 'tolerance' shifted focus and direction as a discourse. Instead of being primarily a domestic discourse concerned with multiculturalism, suddenly the United States became, in political discourse, identified with being a tolerant nation and the West became identified as a tolerant civilization. The 'enemy' was conceived as intolerant, authoritarian, or otherwise barbaric. Instead of just having the tolerating magnanimous host and the tolerated subject, now we have something else: we have a discourse in which there is the tolerant West and the intolerant East, or tolerant Christianity contrasted with the intolerant world of Islam.

What is interesting about the way *that* works is that the tolerant West understands itself as relentlessly tolerant, and nothing but tolerant, in relationship to a picture it draws of another civilization, as relentlessly intolerant. Now, one of the things that is wrong with that picture is that the West, of course, has a history of crusades and slavery and Nazism and all kinds of other things which are just whitewashed by this discourse. The other problem is that this self-portrait by the West literally permits a kind of cultural and civilizational supremacy that licenses a certain kind of imperialism. We are tolerant, we are for tolerance, and we have to exterminate intolerance wherever we find it. We practise tolerance until we come up against the so-called intolerant, at which point we are allowed to topple it, or launch an imperial war against it, or other such things. So one of the worries I developed about the early period of the twenty-first century was the way that our commitment to tolerance was actually being used to underwrite imperial wars.

NW: *Surely America just is more tolerant than, for instance, Saudi society?*

WB: To some degree, yes. Certainly there is a general commitment to religious freedom and other liberties, principles of the sort enshrined in the Constitution and also accepted by, let's say, 75 per cent of Americans. Certainly there is a practice and value of tolerance that we associate with American society that we don't associate with select practices of Islamic religion and some Islamic societies. Once we have said that, though, we have a problem. Tolerance is not simply being declared as a good thing; it is being declared as our *essence* and their lack. It is being depicted as governing and saturating us, absent in them. And that is where there is simply a falsehood being circulated.

American society is not relentlessly tolerant, and the very people using tolerance to launch certain kinds of wars—and I have in mind here the Bush–Cheney administration—are proudly intolerant in certain other respects. Moreover, what is worrisome here is that tolerance is being used as a justification for not tolerating another regime, culture, or religion. Tolerance isn't just a discourse of power, it is also a discourse of conditionality; that is to say, you will be tolerated unless and until you behave in certain ways, at which point I will no longer tolerate you. That is the way tolerance discourse was being used in the post-9/11 period: it was being used to anoint the West as inherently and essentially tolerant, which then justified our intolerance of anything we designated as intolerable. I know this sounds tautological but that is exactly the way the logic of tolerance works in its civilizational mode.

NW: *But surely every political term is loaded. If we use the term 'freedom', we mean 'freedom in certain respects'. If we use 'equality', we have to specify equality of what.*

WB: That is right. The difference is, I think, that most people—even people not in academic fields of political philosophy or other kinds of social criticism—know that about 'freedom' and 'equality'. We know that these words are protean; they shift their meanings in different discourses and in different political systems. We know that 'freedom' and 'equality' also tend to carry problems of power with them. We rarely defend notions of absolute freedom or absolute equality and we argue a lot about both their nature and their relation. In other words, there is a known complexity that goes along with these terms and a known need to investigate: what do you mean in a particular case by equality? Do you mean social equality? Economic equality? Political equality? Legal? Formal? And so on. Tolerance doesn't tend to get that scrutiny. It more often tends to be treated as an inherent good, one that is warm and pleasant, which is an alternative to nightmarish wars, persecution, death, or terrible strictures in societies. What I am suggesting is that we need to give it exactly the kind of scrutiny that we give those other terms.

What worries me about the way that tolerance has come to operate in the last couple of decades in the West is that, in addition to being a civilizational discourse, it is often a substitute for projects of egalitarianism and freedom. It sometimes represents a retrenchment from those more substantive projects or a gloss for their absence. One of the things I am aiming to do is call attention to the fact that tolerance is not equality, it is not freedom. It is something else.

METAPHYSICS AND MIND

II

A. W. MOORE ON
Infinity

David Edmonds: *Can God cook a breakfast so big He can't eat it? That's just one of the paradoxes thrown up by the troubling concept of infinity. Professor A. W. Moore is at Oxford University: his knowledge of the infinite knows no bounds.*

Nigel Warburton: *Now the topic we're going to talk about is infinity. What exactly is infinity?*

A. W. Moore: There are two reasons why that's a difficult question right from the outset. One problem, or basic paradox, that arises with infinity is that it arguably can't be defined—almost by definition.

The point about the infinite is that it resists being pinned down, and if you're trying to define the concept, then what you're trying to do is pin it down in some way, circumscribe it, give it parameters. And a lot of people say: 'Well, that's exactly what you can't do with the infinite; you can't define it.'

Then there's another problem, which is not quite so peculiar to infinity: it's a problem that would arise with defining a lot of philosophical concepts. It's the problem that there hasn't been much of a consensus. If you look back over the thousands of years that people have been discussing the infinite, you'll see that they've had very different views about what it is. So if we were to venture some definition of the infinite, we would automatically be taking sides in the debate.

But one way of approaching it is to compare it with the finite. How does infinity compare with finitude? The answer, in some ways, is very basic. Anything that's finite can be contrasted with something else. It may be that we're talking about literal spatial finitude: for example, a physical object which is finitely big, or which has certain spatial parameters, such as a chair or a table. Precisely because it occupies a certain fixed amount of space, it can be contrasted with other things that are outside that space and that are independent of it. So a contrast between the infinite and the finite appears to be that the infinite doesn't stand *opposed* to anything else. The infinite embraces everything.

But once again, this means we're dealing with a basic paradox, because, on the one hand, the idea is that the infinite doesn't stand opposed to anything else—it is all-inclusive—while on the other hand, precisely what that is, is a way of contrasting the infinite with the finite. By definition, you can't contrast the infinite with the finite, although that's exactly what you want to do.

NW: *Infinity crops up in different areas of thought. In school, people encounter infinity in mathematics. Presumably*

*mathematicians have had to be reasonably precise about what they
mean by infinity.*

AWM: You're right; and for many people that is their first
encounter with the infinite. Think about ordinary whole
numbers: 1, 2, 3, 4, 5, etc., where the crucial thing is the 'etc.'.
It's not long before children arrive at the idea that this is a
sequence that can never end. However big a number you
think of, there's always the possibility of thinking of an even
bigger number.

One of the ways in which mathematicians try to sharpen
this idea is with reference to yet more paradoxes. Suppose
that you're interested in deciding whether one set of objects
is the same size as another set. For example, you might want
to know whether the number of people that live on your
street is the same as the number of dogs that there are on
your street. Now, one way of deciding that is to count them.
If you count the people living on your street, and it turns out
there are twenty-seven, and if you then count the dogs that
there are on your street, and it turns out there are twenty-
seven, lo and behold, there's an answer to your question.
There is the same number of people as dogs.

But sometimes you can tell that two sets are the same
size without counting. You might not have the resources to
count. Suppose you go to some football match at which
there's a huge crowd of people—too many to count—and
suppose you consider the question whether the number of
left legs in the stadium is the same as the number of right
legs. Assuming you know that there isn't some unfortunate
person who's missing a leg, you can immediately answer
that question without bothering to count. You don't have

to work out how many legs there are. You know that
the number of left legs is the same as the number of right
legs, because they can be paired off with each other.
Corresponding to each left leg there's that person's right
leg, and vice versa.

That seems to be a basic way of comparing sets in size. But
if you think about what happens when you're dealing with
infinite sets, again there's a paradox. Suppose we think once
again about the positive whole numbers—1, 2, 3, 4, 5,
etc.—and suppose we also think specifically about the ones
that are even—2, 4, 6, 8, 10, etc. Now, on the face of it, we're
inclined to say there are fewer even numbers than there are
numbers altogether. There are all those odd numbers as well!
And yet, going back to the example of left legs and right legs,
we can perform a similar sort of trick. We can pair off all the
numbers with those that are specifically even, in the obvious
way: 1 gets paired with 2, 2 gets paired with 4, 3 gets paired
with 6, and so on and so forth. It looks as if we have to say
that there are just as many even numbers as there are
numbers altogether, because they can be paired off in this
way. So it's a paradox; it's puzzling.

But rather than be fazed by this paradox, what mathematicians do is put it to their advantage. This comes right back to
your original question, about how mathematicians clarify
the infinite. What mathematicians do is to use this paradox
as their way of explaining what the infinite *is*. They say that
a collection or set of objects is infinite precisely when this
sort of paradox arises. If you can pair off a sub-collection
with the whole collection in the way that we just have done,
that means you're talking about an infinite collection of
objects.

NW: *From a psychological point of view, this is mind-boggling. That's a common feature of the infinite. There's a stage at which you start to realize these paradoxes are all around you.*

AWM: It *is* mind-boggling; there's no doubt about it. Psychologically, it's very difficult to get your mind around these things. Mathematicians try to take these paradoxes in their stride. Philosophers and non-mathematicians tend to be more puzzled. Let's think about these numbers again. It's all very well a mathematician saying that it makes perfectly good mathematical sense, but in non-mathematical terms it really does seem to be puzzling. The German mathematician David Hilbert (1862–1943) used to lecture on these topics, and would illustrate these paradoxes in a very striking way. He imagined a hotel, which subsequently got referred to as 'Hilbert's hotel', which was unlike any normal hotel in that it had infinitely many rooms in it. He would ask his audience to imagine that one cold, dark, wet, windy night somebody turns up, desperate for accommodation. He's not booked in. He's hoping that he can get in at the last moment; he's hoping that there will be a spare room available. And, to his intense disappointment, he finds out that all the rooms in this hotel, even though it's infinite, are occupied. There are infinitely many guests who have already checked in for the night.

He's bitterly disappointed. But then the receptionist has a brainwave. She says, 'With a little bit of juggling, we may be able to accommodate you after all.' So she gets in touch with all the guests. She says to the guest in Room 1, 'Would you mind transferring to Room 2?' He says, 'That's fine.' She says to the guest in Room 2, 'Would you mind transferring to

Room 3?' He says, 'No problem.' And so on. Everybody moves along one: because there are infinitely many rooms, that's possible. So everybody shifts along one, and they're all still accommodated. But Room 1 is now vacant and this visitor can check in for the night!

NW: *I can see that the concept of infinity throws up a number of fun and intriguing puzzles and paradoxes—but why do you think we are so interested in the infinite?*

AWM: That is in many ways *the* crucial question. And the answer has to do with something that you touched on right at the beginning: the basic contrast between the infinite and the finite, and in particular between the infinite and our own finitude.

In all sorts of ways, we ourselves are finite. Obviously, we're physically finite: we only take up a finite amount of space. Even more basically, we only take up a finite amount of time. Each of us has a finite history, and there will come a time when we don't exist any longer. But in other, more metaphorical ways we're finite as well. We're limited: we're limited in what we can do, and we're limited in what we can know. I think our fascination with the infinite comes from a vague sense that there is something out there that contrasts with our own finitude. We feel that we must be part of something much bigger. We are constrained; we are limited. But what's out there—whatever form it may take, whatever it might be like—is ultimately unconstrained, and unlimited. Even if it turns out that the universe is physically finite, or even if it turns out that space and time themselves are finite—which is what a lot of physicists these days suggest—nevertheless

there remains this metaphorical sense in which there's
something there which is unconditioned or unlimited, in stark
contrast to us.

The fascination with the infinite is part of that general
fascination that human beings have with their own place in
the wider scheme of things. How do we fit in? What is the
relationship between this little finite chunk of reality which
is me, and all the rest of it?

NW: *And historically, most philosophers who got interested in the
infinite were talking not just about an abstract mathematical concept
but about the nature of God.*

AWM: That's right. The infinite has always been of
philosophical interest. Western philosophy, going right back
to the pre-Socratics, over 2,500 years ago, has always had a
fascination with the infinite. As you quite rightly say,
historically there's been more emphasis on those more
metaphysical aspects of the infinite—in particular, as part of
a preoccupation with God—than the more mathematical
aspects that we were considering earlier.

NW: *You've written a book that is probably the definitive work on
infinity. What conclusions did you come to?*

AWM: Well, first of all, it's very kind of you to describe my
book in that way. My own focus was largely historical. We
were just talking about how the concept has been of interest
in the history of philosophy, ever since its beginning. One of
the conclusions that I came to is that it is a fundamental
philosophical concept. It's no accident that all the great
philosophers have had something to say about it. When

you're thinking about the infinite, you're thinking about something very basic. It's a supremely important philosophical concept, but it's also riddled with paradoxes, as we've seen. One of the things I tried to do in that book was to see how we could have our cake and eat it: continue to acknowledge the importance of the infinite, on the one hand, and on the other hand take seriously all the paradoxes that afflict it and all the difficulties we confront when we try to talk about it.

12

DAVID PAPINEAU ON
Scientific Realism

David Edmonds: *Most scientists now believe that there are unobservable entities in the world. These entities can't be seen, touched, smelt, or felt. In that sense, they're not like ordinary objects: tables or tomatoes or television sets. But, at least according to scientific realists, they're just as real as tables or tomatoes or television sets. David Papineau is a tangible professor of King's College London.*

Nigel Warburton: *We are focusing on scientific realism. Could you just explain what scientific realism is?*

David Papineau: Scientific realism is the view that the world as described by scientific theories really exists and we know about that world. In particular it is concerned with the world of unobservables: the world of electrons and atoms, molecules, viruses, radio waves, and so on—things that we can't see or otherwise sense. So whether we really do know them to exist or not is a contentious issue. In the area of philosophy of science, scepticism is a serious option: many philosophers of science hold that, while there no doubt *is* an unobservable world, we have no way of finding out about it. This contrasts with the philosophy of everyday medium-sized physical objects. There we talk about scepticism in *Philosophy 101*, but this is just an exercise. There the question is: 'How can we refute the sceptic?' But nobody really thinks that we don't know about tables and chairs and everyday objects. However, in philosophy of science quite a lot of serious people think we *really* don't know about the unobservable world, and they believe that scientific theories are just convenient, useful myths that aren't reporting on reality.

NW: *So the sceptic says that unobservable things, which scientists talk about, are actually convenient fictions, whereas the realist says these things actually exist?*

DP: Exactly, and this issue has a very interesting history. At the start of the Scientific Revolution—with Descartes, Boyle, and running up to Newton—the scientists were serious realists about the observable world. They were very optimistic. In fact the defining characteristic of the Scientific Revolution was that its adherents were mechanical philosophers. They thought the whole world was a machine. Observable things were composed of lots of small little bits, and it was the behaviour of the bits, their interactions, that explained what we observed. And they set out to try and figure out what these bits were. They were materialists: they thought the whole world was made up of complicated arrangements of matter.

The trouble was that in the seventeenth century they didn't get very far. They found out quite a lot of interesting things—for example, that air exerts pressure and if you go up a mountain the pressure reduces—but they found it difficult to figure out the mechanism responsible for that. They weren't sure whether the air was made of little springs like you get inside a biro, or some kind of elastic solid that you could walk through, or whatever—and they didn't have any clue about how to resolve this. Newton figured out that gravity obeyed the inverse square law, but when the question arose, 'exactly why do bodies move in this way?', no mechanistic explanation could be derived. Newton himself famously said *'Hypotheses non fingo'*, 'I feign no hypotheses', by which he meant that he thought it wasn't the proper business of science to speculate about all these unobservable mechanisms—and speculation is what he thought it would have to be. This is a perfectly natural point of view. How could we possibly figure out that tables or bits of wood are made up of all these tiny particles that behave in such-and-such specific ways? It is completely flabbergasting that we now take ourselves to know such things. This was the view that came to be adopted after the best part of a century of trying. From the eighteenth century onwards the scientists gave up and came to regard any such microscopic hypothesizing as perhaps interesting speculation, but certainly not seriously-to-be-believed theory.

NW: *So you are saying that scepticism arose principally through the failures of science?*

DP: Absolutely; and, as I have just explained, it seems to me a perfectly natural position to adopt, especially in the absence of any convincing serious scientific theories of the relevant kind—in other words, any serious theories of unobservables.

NW: *What happened in the nineteenth century to change all this?*

DP: Well, what happened is that for the first time some serious testable theories were put forward about the unobservable microscopic mechanisms responsible for what we observe. In particular there was the atomic theory of matter—which developed as people got clear about chemistry and the difference between elements and compounds and mixtures, and the laws of constant combination by mass and volume. If you think about that, the natural explanation to give is that bits of matter are made of little particles that combine in certain simple whole-number ratios. And then that combined with the kinetic theory of gases and the kinetic theory of heat. So by the end of the nineteenth century there was an overwhelming amount of evidence in favour of the atomic theory. The philosophers and the philosophical scientists were still persuaded by Newton that this couldn't be serious, but it became so manifestly serious that slowly the working scientists all joined up and by the early twentieth century they had all become realists. They thought it must be possible to find out about the unobservable world—because we manifestly have succeeded in doing so. Of course a few philosophers remained unpersuaded.

NW: *Essentially what these scientists were doing was hypothesizing about causes on the basis of visible effects.*

DP: Exactly. And that leaves a couple of openings for philosophers who aren't convinced of scientific realism to remain sceptics. Interestingly, they don't nowadays call themselves sceptics. They use a numbers of terms—they call themselves instrumentalists, or empiricists, or constructive empiricists. In truth, all these people who have doubts about scientific knowledge of the unobservable world are just sceptics—although adding perhaps a little bit about how the theories are useful instruments for making predictions, useful for suggesting new research, and so on. But basically they agree with the eighteenth- and the early nineteenth-century scientists that knowledge of the unobservable world is not possible.

NW: *So why exactly do they think that?*

DP: Well, there are two powerful and pretty influential arguments against scientific realism. One is the argument from the underdetermination of theory by evidence: the thought here is that, given any set of observable phenomena, there will always be a number of alternative explanations for those phenomena. So imagine the phenomena of light— angle of incidence equals angle of reflection, the law of refraction (Snell's Law)—all those things can be explained either by the wave theory of light or, given a little bit of work, by the particle theory of light. So you have got two different explanations, two different possible causes, for the same observable phenomena. How do you decide between them? You can't, the sceptic says. So that is the argument from the underdetermination of theory by evidence.

The other argument is called 'pessimistic meta-induction from past falsity'. Sorry if that sounds a bit of a mouthful, but it is easy enough to understand. It is the argument that says that, if you look at past scientific theories, they all turn out to be wrong, so our present theories are probably wrong too. You can see it is pessimistic and it is a meta-induction because

it is inducing from the past failures of science to present
failures.

NW: *Okay, let's take those one at a time. First the underdetermina-*
tion of theory by the data. That sounds quite plausible. You made a good
case for it with the example of light. There are two alternative explana-
tions, both of which fit the observable facts.

DP: Good. But it is not as powerful an argument as it looks
at first sight. Those two theories—the wave theory and the
particle theory—they are both on the cards, given the initial
data. The initial data can be explained equally well by both
those theories. But in most cases—and, in particular, in this
case—it is possible to figure out some prediction that is made
by one of the theories and not by the other. And then you can
test it. That is called a crucial experiment. In this case, the
wave theory predicts that you will observe certain interference phenomena in certain situations and the particle theory
doesn't have any natural explanation of that. When we try it,
we find interference patterns. So the particle theory is out,
and the wave theory wins. Now that doesn't fully settle the
underdetermination-by-evidence argument, because one can
always come up with some other theory that will once more,
alongside the wave theory, explain all the phenomena,
including the interference phenomena.

For example, here are a couple of silly theories. One says
that there isn't any unobservable world, there is just the
observable world, and it just so happens that in certain
situations you observe interference phenomena. So that is a
kind of 'atheistic' theory of the data—there is nothing behind
the observable world. Here is another theory: there are lots

of little green men running around, much too small to see, and they are arranging everything in just such a way as to make the wave theory look right. Now those are both coherent and consistent theories, and they explain the data. But of course nobody takes them at all seriously. In effect, to argue from those kinds of theories is just to say that it is never possible to infer anything that goes beyond the evidence, and *that* in other contexts is not a principle that is adopted, and it shouldn't be adopted in science. So the truth is that, given any two serious theories, you can normally decide between them by doing some more experiments. Then you will be left with some crackpot theories, but I don't think anybody should seriously think that crackpot theories undermine our knowledge of the atomic theory of matter, say, or the wave theory of light.

NW: *So what you are saying is, usually when there are two competing theories, running side by side, it is not that both are in a sense true or anything like that. There is a right answer; it's just that we haven't quite worked out how to find out the crucial experiment that will decide what it is. But when we do decide it, science moves on. We ditch one of the theories. The trouble is that then you have got this pattern of rejecting theories over and over again—each theory is set up to be knocked down.*

DP: Right. So that brings us to the other argument, that is, the pessimistic meta-induction from past falsity. They aren't complementary arguments. Interestingly, sceptics about scientific knowledge tend to run either one or the other. You can see why: the underdetermination argument is that there are too many good theories; whereas the pessimistic meta-induction argument is that there are too few good theories—in fact there aren't any.

So we should turn to the second argument. That is a very serious argument. If past theories all turn out to be false then it would be foolish to feel that somehow our present theories must be true. So realists have a number of options. One thing they might do is say: 'Look, the past theories aren't just outright false: they were wrong in a few details, but basically they had a lot of truth and they were approximately true.' For example, the wave theory of matter isn't exactly right, because now with quantum theory we know that light moves in wave-like particles—photons. But still, the fact that light obeys the equations of wave motion and so on—that was all okay—so the theory was approximately true.

NW: *Is approximate truth good enough for realism? Is it good enough to say something really is there, if we are just approximating?*

DP: Well realism, *schmealism*. If realism is supposed to be the view that our current scientific theories are *exactly* true, *that* realism is no good. But we have a position that says our current scientific theories no doubt have an awful lot of truth in them, and we have every entitlement to be confident about that. Perhaps that is not the realism that you might have hoped for in the first place—but given the evidence of past scientific theories, it looks like the right position to adopt.

NW: *But this isn't a historical relativism about scientific truth, is it?*

DP: No, no, just the opposite. Relativism would be the position you would adopt if you were persuaded by the pessimistic meta-induction: each historical period's theories were believed by the people of the time, but from a more objective, timeless point of view you could see that all these theories had no real authority, they were all out of tune with what reality was like. So people *thought* they were right but they weren't, or aren't. That is the relativist point of view. The point of view of the realist who resists the pessimistic meta-induction is that all these theories have some good truth in them—not every detail of the theory, but lots of truth—and that builds up, and we should trust what the scientists say to that extent.

NW: *Does that then mean that there can't be scientific revolutions in which the whole way of doing science is radically transformed?*

DP: Well, if you bought the story about approximate truth that would mean there are no scientific revolutions: new theories get built on the old ones. But I haven't yet given you convincing reasons to support that view. If you look at the history of science, there are plenty of cases which don't seem to fit the approximate-truth story. If you think of classical mechanics, Newton being replaced by Einstein, well in some ways what Newton's theories said were approximately true—for example, what Newton says about objects at low velocities. On the other hand, what the theory says about objects moving at velocities close to the speed of light is wildly wrong. So there the realist probably has to adopt a different strategy. What a realist should say is that the original pessimistic meta-induction is just too crude, even if you put to one side the issues of approximate truth.

There are some areas in which it seems that new theories *do* often radically overthrow old ones. For example, when we look at general theories of space-time cosmology, we do seem to get these kinds of revolutions. The moral is that we should take current cosmological theories with a pinch of salt. We have current general relativity, big bang, and so on—but it is quite possible that in fifty years' time we will think reality has thirteen dimensions and what we observe is just a low-energy four-dimensional projection of it, and it will seem to us that what we currently believe is all wrong.

But one shouldn't infer from that, that the atomic theory of matter is all wrong. There are cases and cases. There are some areas of science—I mentioned general cosmology, but I could add psychology and certain parts of social science—where there are all these flip-flops all the time. And then there are other areas of science—chemistry, parts of engineering—where people build steadily on the past theories. The moral is obvious: there are some areas of science where we *can* have a high degree of credence in the theories and other areas of science where we ought to be pretty sceptical.

NW: *We should be sceptics about some areas of science, and realists about others?*

DP: Absolutely. And if you think that I am giving up on what I promised you earlier—scientific realism—well that is too bad, because it seems to me the position I have outlined is obviously the sensible one. If you think about the question in the first place: 'Should we be realists about *science*, about everything put forward by people who claim the authority of scientists?' Well, why should we? We should be realists about good theories and we should be sceptical about dodgy ones.

NW: *The difficulty, of course, is finding out which are good and which are dodgy.*

DP: Yes, right. So one thing I have pointed to is past track record in different areas of science. Cosmology doesn't have that great a track record, but post-1800 chemistry has a terrific track record. But one might try and back that up by looking at something else, which is maybe the *reason* some areas have a good track record and other ones don't. Some areas have plenty of evidence and other areas are working with very thin evidence. Here is another example: palaeo-anthropology, the history of the evolution of the hominid lineage over the past 5 million years. People keep on chang-ing their minds—once it was that we descended from *Australopithecus*—and that was all wrong—and now we have got five new species. This is because they are struggling with a few bits of tooth and bone to figure out a lot of detailed stuff from 5 million years ago. So it is not surprising that they are guessing. Contrast this with the wealth of evidence that developed in the nineteenth century: chemical combinations, kinetic theory, and so on. If you go and look at all that evidence, it would be very, very difficult not to be completely convinced of the atomic theory. This difference in track record reflects another thing which gives us independent reason to be more serious about some theories than others—namely, that some theories have a lot more evidence in their favour than others.

NW: *The example you just gave was a historical one—about something that happened in the past. But if we are doing history you could say there is just not enough evidence to decide between competing theories. Nonetheless, most people are going to say, well surely something really did happen nevertheless. There is a truth to the matter, even if we don't know what it is.*

DP: Good, yes. So that takes us back to the beginning. I have been articulating the strengths and weaknesses of scientific realism, by which I mean not just the view that there is an independent reality, but that plus the view that we can *know* about it. The view that there is an independent reality and we can't know about it is scepticism. So of course there is a fact of the matter about what happened in the past, including what happened in the palaeoanthropological past, but the interesting issue here, which is the one we are debating, is, can we *find out* about it?

NW: *Just to round this up, it sounds to me as if what you are saying is that the history of science is actually the history of getting closer to the truth.*

DP: Well, I did qualify that by saying in some areas it is not obvious that that is so—but in other areas, yes it is. I would like to invoke a very fine Australian philosopher, David Stove. Stove said, look at what we have discovered, look at what we know about chemistry, look at what we know about diseases, look at what we know about engineering— people who say that all scientific theories are no doubt false is talking through their hat. And that is what I think too.

13

BARRY STROUD ON
Scepticism

David Edmonds: *Can I really know anything? If so, what can I know? Epistemology—the study of knowledge—is a central concern in philosophy. A sceptic says we can know nothing, or next-to-nothing. Barry Stroud—Professor of Philosophy at the University of California at Berkeley—isn't a full-blown sceptic. But it's common knowledge that he's a leading authority on scepticism.*

Nigel Warburton: *The topic I want to ask you about is scepticism. In a sense, all philosophers are sceptics in that they doubt things. Could you say what you understand by scepticism?*

Barry Stroud: The kind of scepticism I am interested in arises out of a very general philosophical enterprise: the attempt to understand in general how human knowledge of the world around us is possible. This can become a pressing problem because there are various familiar considerations which, when generalized, seem to count against the possibility of any knowledge of the world at all. And trying to show how those obstacles can be overcome turns out to be more difficult than it might have seemed. Scepticism is the conclusion that those obstacles cannot be overcome and that we cannot really know anything about the world.

NW: *I can see you now, you're sitting in front of me. It's hard to be sceptical about your existence. Could you elaborate a little bit on where the difficulties lie with that kind of perceptual encounter that we're having?*

BS: I think that is the right way to pose the question, because I believe the real source of the kind of scepticism I am interested in lies in a certain understanding of perception, of how you actually do see me, or what kind of knowledge you can have of my presence on the basis of what you now see. This, of course, is the way Descartes raised the problem in the seventeenth century.

NW: *Descartes entertained sceptical arguments in order to get to something which he thought was the bedrock on which he could build his edifice of knowledge. So, in a sense, he was a pre-emptive sceptic: he was getting the sceptics before they got him. He argued that the senses are notoriously unreliable, so that just because I think I see you in front of me it doesn't follow that you really are in front of me.*

BS: Yes. It was part of Descartes's task to get the senses out of the picture as a source of knowledge; to show that they are not the source of knowledge that people have supposed them to be. As you have just said, one way to challenge the senses as a source of knowledge is to point out that they are not necessarily reliable. We can go wrong by relying on our senses. Descartes mentions that. But it seems equally true that we also rely on our senses to check up on our senses: we can undo some of the mistakes we might have made earlier.

So Descartes's doubts about the reliability of the senses do not ultimately rest simply on the fact that sometimes the senses lead us astray.

Where I live, by the sea in California, the weather is very mild. When I go out in the morning my car starts every time. But if I go up into the mountains in the winter and try to start my car in the morning, I cannot rely on it starting every time. The conditions under which I am trying to start it are different. I know that, and it doesn't make me conclude that my car is generally unreliable. Descartes says the same thing about the senses. I can sometimes go wrong on the basis of the senses alone when things are too far away, for instance, or when they are close but too small to be seen properly. But that does not make me think that I can never rely on the senses, even when clearly visible things are in front of me in the light of day. But there *are* considerations that do seem to bring into doubt the reliability of the senses in general for finding out anything about the world.

NW: *So, what are those considerations?*

BS: Well, suppose it could be shown that on each and every occasion on which I take myself to be perceiving that something or other is so in the world, I could be perceiving what I perceive on that occasion *even though the world I think I am perceiving is not in fact the way it seems to me to be*. One possibility of this that Descartes does not mention, but others have mentioned, is that whenever I have a perception of something I am actually having a hallucination. So things in the world would not really be the way they seem to me to be. That perhaps raises the question whether you could be hallucinating all the time, or whether a hallucination is something that can occur only some of the time.

What Descartes himself introduces is the possibility that you are dreaming. That is certainly something familiar to all of us. When we dream it seems to us at the time that we are, say, walking along beside the river, whereas we are in fact lying in a dark room in bed. Perceptually, it is exactly as if I am walking by the river, but I am not. So to know that I *am* walking by the river, even when I am actually walking there, it seems as if I would have to find some reason to believe that I am not dreaming. Can I ever dismiss the possibility that I am merely dreaming that I am by the river on the basis of anything I could perceive at that moment?

NW: *So he's looking for some kind of marker that indicates that the present perceptions are genuinely of the world and not of a dream.*

BS: That's a good way to put it, in terms of a 'marker' or some recognizable feature of my perception. And the problem is that whatever could be present in my perception that might seem to indicate to me that I am not dreaming seems to be something that could also be present in any dream experience. For example, suppose I was told that when you are looking at something and see a little red dot in the lower right-hand corner of your visual field, this is an indication that you are not dreaming. The red dot is the sign of reality. Well, surely there is nothing to prevent you from dreaming and finding a little red dot in the lower right-hand corner of your dream experience.

NW: *Now, that seems pretty powerful. Do you think he was right that every experience could in principle be contained within a dream?*

BS: That is a huge and complicated question. In fact, there are two different questions here. Is it possible for there to be something in one's perceptual experience at a given moment that could reliably indicate to you that you are not dreaming at that moment? That's one question. Many people who see the force of this consideration—as you do—would say no, there could not. But some would go on to say that that is okay because you do not have to know that you are not dreaming at a particular moment in order to have perceptual knowledge of the world at that time. That is because knowing that you are not dreaming is not required in general in order for you to have reliable perceptual knowledge of the world.

NW: *So, I'm dreaming that I'm in this room talking to you—or I might be dreaming that—and I don't know at the moment whether I'm dreaming or not: how can I then be sure that I have some knowledge of anything beyond the dream?*

BS: Well, this second line of defence that I have distinguished says that you do not have to know that you're not dreaming in order to know by perception what is going on around you. As long as you actually are perceiving what's going on around you, and it is connected in the right way with your perceiving it, then you do or can know what is so. That is to say, you can satisfy the conditions of knowing how things are in the world—so you know—even though it is not a condition of knowing something that you know that you know it. There are things we know that perhaps we don't know that we know. But that does not mean that we do not know them.

So this diagnosis says that the sceptical conclusion that we don't know anything about the world rests on a faulty or unjustified assumption. It assumes that if you do not know that you know a certain thing, then you do not know it. This response says that is a misconception of the nature of knowledge.

NW: *We've got quite abstract. We're engaging in philosophical debate, and somebody who's not a philosopher will say: 'I know I'm not dreaming, so what's the point of discussing a case like this?'*

BS: Well, yes. The abstraction or generality of the discussion raises a question about the nature or the point of this philosophical enterprise. You could think of philosophy in this respect as a kind of very high-level anthropology. It's as if we try to stand back and look at human beings in general and see how they function. We see them and we see the world that they operate in, and we want to understand how they have knowledge of that world. And we see that sense perception is obviously very important for knowledge. But human beings also have many other concerns in life, like getting on and living with one another, and so on. So knowledge is not the only thing human beings are interested in—thank goodness. But that does not mean that whenever things go smoothly with people saying things and accepting and relying on the things that others say, they really do know the things they think they do. We have not necessarily understood whether or how human beings actually know the sorts of things they think they do, or whether they just happen to get some things right about the way things are.

Knowing something is not the same thing as believing something and its being true. You can have true beliefs and not know the things in question; you could make a lucky guess, for example. If someone flips a coin and one person thinks it is going to be heads and another thinks it is going to be tails, one of them has to be right, but neither of them knows. So, if we distinguish knowledge from true belief and see that it involves something more, the question is, what is that something more? And is this 'something more' present in what we ordinarily take to be cases of knowledge? That is what is in question in this kind of philosophical enterprise. If I do see something, and the world is actually the way I see it to be, that does not by itself give me knowledge on this conception of knowledge because I might just happen to be perceiving something that is exactly the way things are. In order to have knowledge, I have to see that things are the way they are and in some sense *know* that they are that way, and that's where the problem comes from.

NW: *So another way of looking at this is that the philosophical enterprise of investigating sceptical arguments in this way is actually an attempt to understand the human condition: we're trying to get an overview of just how we relate to the world.*

BS: That's right, and it is very important. That is the kind of enterprise I am calling a completely general anthropological investigation of the human species. In everyday life, we are concerned with finding out certain things and getting on with people, and whether we have knowledge or not is not always the primary concern. But in the philosophical enterprise of understanding knowledge, those more practical concerns are put to one side for the moment. We want to gain a certain kind of detached intellectual understanding of a fundamental aspect of human life. What we really want to understand is part of the human condition: what does it take for human beings to be knowers of the world around them, and do they succeed?

NW: *As a philosopher, you are almost obliged to be a sceptic to some degree, or at least to entertain sceptical arguments—because otherwise you're just a dogmatist, presumably. Is that a fair assessment?*

BS: As a philosopher you try to understand various aspects of the human condition, and you try to do that while presupposing as little as possible yourself. You don't want to take any more for granted than you have to for the purpose at hand. But that kind of caution or doubt is not the kind of scepticism that appears to be the outcome of this philosophical enterprise. The scepticism that comes out of this enterprise is much stronger than that. It is not just a matter of doubting or being cautious or not taking many things for granted. It is the paradoxical conclusion that nobody knows anything about the world around them.

Now in that sense, almost no philosophers are sceptics. I think the considerations that seem to lead to that sceptical conclusion are powerful and still not correctly understood. My zeal in drawing attention to the force of those arguments has led some people to think of me as a defender of scepticism. That of course is absurd; it would mean that I think nobody knows anything about the world at all. But I do think that trying to get to the bottom of the considerations that seem to lead to that sceptical conclusion, and trying to find out how and why that conclusion cannot be reached, or even what the obstacles are to reaching it, would be a great contribution to the understanding of one fundamental aspect of the human condition. That is the kind of interest it has for me.

14

HUGH MELLOR ON
Time

David Edmonds: *I'm writing this cue now. In a couple of minutes I'll have finished it—my writing of it will have been done, past. Hopefully, in the future, after you've read this introduction, you'll be reading an interview with Hugh Mellor, Emeritus Professor of Philosophy at Cambridge University. Professor Mellor believes that 'tense'—the past, the present, the future—is not part of time per se. Your reading of this introduction will precede your reading of the interview: things happen earlier and later. But Professor Mellor argues time itself is not essentially tensed. Confused? Hopefully, in ten minutes, you'll be less so. Hugh Mellor took time out to talk to* Philosophy Bites.

Nigel Warburton: *The topic we are focusing on today is time. It's quite easy to see why physicists would be interested in time and its measurement, but why philosophers?*

Hugh Mellor: Time has always posed problems that interest philosophers, and indeed some physicists for philosophical reasons: like whether it flows, and whether it's something in itself or just, so to speak, something that separates events that happen one after the other. The relation between time and space is another question that interests both physicists and philosophers.

NW: *To me that sounds almost like science: whether time flows sounds like an empirical question.*

HM: It sounds like an empirical question, but it really isn't, although it's something physicists have occasionally taken for granted. Isaac Newton took it for granted: he said that time in itself flows equably without regard essentially to what happens in it—so you could have time without anything in it. But whether that's so or not, it's really a philosophical question; it's one on which Newton pursued a long controversy with the German philosopher and mathematician Gottfried Wilhelm Leibniz.

NW: *Your book* Real Time, *and its successor,* Real Time II, *both deal with the question of tense. Could you say a little bit about what tense is and how it relates to time?*

HM: Tense, in its normal, non-philosophical usage, simply refers to a variation in the form of verbs depending on whether you're talking about the past, the present, or the future: something *happened*, something *is* happening, something *will* happen. But as used by philosophers talking about time, it doesn't refer to the form of verbs, but to what those verbs are used to discuss: namely past, present, and future as different regions of time. That's what we philosophers mean by tense; it doesn't matter to us whether those regions are referred to using verbs or in some other way. The issues tense raises arise from the fact that things and events—like this interview—appear to move through time.

They start off by being future, which this interview was yesterday, become present, as it is now, and then go on to become past, which it will be in not too short a time.

NW: *That seems quite a natural way of talking about time: we always talk about the past, present, and the future. What's the problem?*

HM: The problem is that while things are past or present or future, none of them stays there. Everything that starts off future becomes present and then becomes past. Although this sounds innocuous enough, in the last century people have realized that it raises a serious problem. For one thing, you don't want to say that events *change* in respect of whether they're past, present, or future. Whatever this interview is *now* must be how it was *yesterday*, or you'd get a contradiction: I can't be saying some things now and it be the case yesterday that I would say something different. I might have *intended* to say something different, but that's another matter: you don't always do what you intend to do.

If I put money on a horse, for example, predicting it will win, and it does win, the now-past fact of its winning must be the same fact as the then-future fact that I put money on; otherwise the bookie could refuse to pay! Whether events are past, present, or future, they have got to be the *same* events. The only way in which they can change is by ceasing to be future by becoming first present and then past. That's quite different from things changing in any other way, like first being hot and then being cold. The question is, how to distinguish this special sort of change.

The best way to start is by noticing that this sort of change has a spatial analogue. For example, at the moment you're not only in Cambridge, you're also *here*, which is where I am. This morning you were in Oxford and at that point you *weren't* here. But the facts of your being in Oxford at one time, and then in Cambridge at a later time, must be the very same facts. And this variation across space, from your being *there* to your being *here*, is exactly analogous to the variation in time, from this interview being *future* to its being *present*. Yet we naturally think that variations over time differ importantly from variations across space in a way that reflects the nature of time itself. The difference is that things flow through time, from future to present, in a way in which things don't (as it were) flow across space, from here to there. The question is, why not and what's the difference?

NW: *So is it fair to say that your view is that tense is another way of describing a relation between a person and an event, but the tense itself doesn't actually exist as part of time?*

HM: The event exists as part of time, but you're right in saying that tense is a relation between a person and an event, like this interview, and relations in general are not properties of what they relate. For example, if, as I suspect, you're taller than me, that fact is not a property of either of us. You yourself are a certain height; I myself am a certain height; and your being taller than me isn't a property of mine, or of yours: it's a relation between us. Similarly, if you say, 'Here I am in Cambridge' now, that statement will be true. But what makes it true isn't that Cambridge or you have the property of being *here*, but that you're saying it *in* Cambridge.

In the same way, while it's true to say 'this interview is happening now', what makes it true is just that it's said during the interview. What makes statements like this true is a relation between what you say—or think—and when you say it. But this 'when', the time at which you say something, isn't in itself either present or past or future. The time just *is*, just as Cambridge just *is*. Suppose, to pursue the spatial analogy, you want to put 'You are here' signs on differently located copies of a map of England. To make what those signs say true, you must put them on correspondingly different parts of that map. On a copy in Cambridge you must make the sign point to the representation of Cambridge, while on a copy of the same map in Oxford you must make the sign point to a representation of Oxford. In other words, the sign on a copy picks out a relation between that copy and its location: namely, the relation of being *at* that location. That's what makes the Oxford and Cambridge signs true, not that either Oxford or Cambridge has the property of being *here*: there's no such property. And so it is with time: this interview doesn't have the property of being *now*, that is, of being *present*, which is acquired when the interview started and will disappear when it ends. There's no such property: the interview simply occurs at a certain time on a certain day. What makes it true to say, during the interview, that it's happening *now* is simply that this statement is made during the interview.

NW: *Why, then, do we talk in tense terms?*

HM: We talk in tense terms because this relation I've been talking about matters very much to when we act and what we do. For example, if I decide to do something—pick something up, or go and fetch something—I will do it at whatever place I'm at or time I'm in. And that will make it true to say or think, as I do it, that I'm doing it *here* and doing it *now*. I don't need to know where I am to know that I'm doing it 'here', any more than I need to know the time at which I do it, to know that I'm doing it 'now'. It's because your 'here' and 'now' automatically follow you around, so to speak, that you can know you're acting in the 'here and now' without knowing whether you're acting in Cambridge or Oxford or at 10 or 11 a.m. And the reason it's absolutely indispensable to think about our actions in these terms is that we have to think of them in a way that fits this relation between our actions and when and where we do them, *not* that they can only occur in places and times that, for some reason, have these mysterious properties of being here and being now.

NW: *Your view, then, is that time is essentially tenseless: there's nothing about past, present, and future built into time?*

HM: No, nothing about past, present, and future is built into time. What is built into time is the difference between *earlier* and *later*, which is the temporal analogue of spatial differences like that between *north* and *south*, say. The reason this temporal difference matters more than its spatial analogue is that other things depend on it that don't depend on the spatial difference. For example, I can't now decide to do something yesterday, because causes, like my deciding to do something, and effects, like my doing it, always precede their effects in time. But they can occur in any direction in space. As far as getting things done goes, there's no funda- mental direction to space. So, for example, while turning on a light-bulb emits light in all directions (and indeed in none, since it lights up the bulb itself), it only lights up things at later times. That's why the direction of time—the difference between later and earlier—matters to us in practice. So when we think of action in tense terms, as we do, we have to distinguish what's future—what's later than when we're thinking about it—from what's earlier—that is, from what we correctly think of as past. That's why these notions matter to us. Only in philosophy is it important to realize that, when we think in this way, we're just reading out into the world what are really just relations between us and parts of it.

NW: *Does it follow from that that you can't go back into an earlier time—so that time travel is somehow conceptually impossible?*

HM: I think it does, though most of my professional colleagues think it doesn't—they think it is indeed possible to travel back in time. Here I'm on the side of people who aren't philosophers—people who think you couldn't go back in time. Because if you could go back in time then you might, for example, kill your grandmother before she has any offspring, thereby making it impossible for you to exist to go back in time in the first place. And while this argument doesn't persuade most philosophers, it does persuade me.

NW: *Why do you think that these issues about time matter so much?*

HM: I'm actually slightly puzzled about that, because I'm not sure they do matter very much. They certainly don't matter in practical terms and I don't think they matter in scientific terms either. That is, our physics will be the same whatever view we take about time. But many physicists think for some reason that there's a puzzle about time. They are not willing to take whatever is measured by clocks, and other devices for measuring time, as just another physical variable like temperature, or indeed distance in space. So a fairly recent issue of the *New Scientist* contained a very silly piece—by someone whose name had better escape me!—about the time 'illusion'. And while there's a long history of respectable physicists and philosophers thinking that time is an illusion, I don't understand why physicists today take this idea to be either new—for example, entailed by quantum physics—or important.

I suspect the idea that time is an illusion arises from a vague sense that there's something odd about tense. And indeed, if you think of tense as a feature of the world, that *is* an illusion, as I've tried to show. What is *not* an illusion is that we are in the world, and need to think about it, and especially about how to act in it, in terms of tense. And the fact that the world requires us to do this shows that time itself—tenseless time, what makes events earlier and later than each other—is indeed a real feature both of the world, and of our experience of it. It's true that not everyone agrees with me about this, for reasons I reject but can at least understand. What I can't understand is why so many intelligent people get so worked up about it: it's on a par with people who think that splitting infinitives is worse than murdering your grandmother!

15

TIM CRANE ON
Mind and Body

David Edmonds: *The central issue in the Philosophy of Mind is how the mind interacts with the body. 'Dualists' maintain that the mind and the body are quite distinct. In the last century the Oxford philosopher Gilbert Ryle ridiculed dualism by evoking an image of the mysterious 'ghost in the machine'. How could this ghost move arms and legs? But other philosophers, such as Thomas Nagel in an oft-quoted article, 'What Is It Like To Be A Bat?', have questioned whether the mind can be reduced to the purely physical. The difficulty is accounting for subjective experience. Could the solution to the mind–body problem lie with scientists? After all, our understanding of the brain is expanding all the time: could neurologists eventually discover how the mind influences the body? Tim Crane, a leading authority on the Philosophy of Mind, thinks not.*

Nigel Warburton: *The topic we want to focus on is mind and body, the relationship between the two. We all know what the body is, but could you say a little bit about what the mind is?*

Tim Crane: The best way to think of this is not to think of the mind as being a thing—some sort of entity that may or may not be separate from the body—but rather to think of human beings as having mental capacities. People have the capacity to think, to act, to feel, and to have emotions and to be conscious: all these mental capacities are the things that I would classify together as the mind.

NW: *You say 'to act'—in the sense of doing things—but why is that mental?*

TC: It's a good question. Why do we classify all the mental things together as the mental at all? I think action is mental because it's intentional, in the sense that it's directed on to something other than itself. So when you act, when you go to buy yourself a coffee, you're aiming at something beyond yourself, namely the result of getting a coffee.

NW: *So it's not just a physical movement?*

TC: I suppose that's the big question: how the mental capacities that we have relate to the physical world—our physical bodies and the rest of the physical world. This is one half of what I think of as the mind–body problem. If our bodies are things in the physical world then moving our bodies changes things in the physical world; it changes the position of physical particles and matter; and we do these things because of what we want, and how we think the world is, and because of our states of consciousness and our emotions, and so on. That gives rise to the conclusion that the mind has effects in the physical world—that mental states and processes have real physical effects in the world. But how can something have effects in the world if it's not physical itself? And that's the part of the mind–body problem which forces you towards what people call materialism or physicalism: the idea that everything is physical or material.

NW: *So what's the other half?*

TC: Well, the other half is when you start thinking of what it would be for the mind to *be* physical. Obviously you look at the brain: the brain is just a few pounds of this watery grey stuff, this rather repulsive fatty substance, and that stuff somehow gives rise to thought, to consciousness, to experience, to emotion, and all the mystery of our inner life. And that's extremely puzzling. So, on the one hand, when we think of how the mind interacts with the physical world, we think it must be something physical. But when we think about consciousness, and in particular the problem of consciousness—how something physical could be conscious—it is completely baffling.

NW: *For the physicalist it's not a problem, is it, because that gooey stuff has all kinds of very complicated chemical electrical relationships going on within it, which actually produce amazingly sophisticated effects? Thinking is current moving in the brain.*

TC: I think that's right, in the sense that that's what a physicalist or materialist should say. But it's one thing to say it, it's another thing to understand it. The American philosopher Thomas Nagel has a brilliant analogy here; somebody who says 'the mind is the brain' now, is in the position of an ancient Greek who said that matter is energy. It's true that matter is energy, but the ancient Greeks who said that wouldn't understand how it could be true; they wouldn't understand what it meant to say that matter was energy.

They could assert that it was true, perhaps; but they wouldn't understand it. Nagel says this is the position we're in with respect to mind and brain. Of course we can say our mental capacities are the product of the brain, but we have no idea how this even could happen—it's baffling.

NW: *I don't understand how a television works. I know it's got all kinds of complex components in there, and I know it's physical. But I don't bring in the idea that there must be something mysteriously working inside the television that's not physical.*

TC: I think there's a difference between the two cases, because although you don't know how the TV works, the scientists who make the TVs know how they work. It's true that scientists know a lot about how the brain works—actually the brain is very well understood at the level of its smallest parts. But what they don't know is what it is about the brain that gives rise to conscious experience. There are different ways of thinking about this. You could think we're just missing that magical part, the Factor 57 or the magic number that we're going to find in the brain. When you press that bit, consciousness lights up. It could be that our position in relation to the brain is one of ignorance. I myself don't believe that. I think that the position that we're in is one of confusion. I think it's a philosophical problem, a philosophical conundrum in which we're confused about what it is that we're trying to understand, rather than simply a question of our ignorance.

NW: *So even if the scientists had a complete map of the brain and understood the way the different parts worked together, you're saying it's* *unlikely, or just impossible, that we would have an understanding of consciousness?*

TC: I don't want to say that, because I think we don't know what understanding of consciousness is. I think that's why we're confused: because we don't know what it is we're trying to explain.

NW: *Are we just trying to clarify the meaning of the word 'conscious-ness' or is there something more that philosophers can do here?*

TC: I don't think we're just trying to clarify the meaning of the word. We're trying to understand the phenomenon of consciousness. And we use whatever resources we can to understand that phenomenon: resources of introspection, of our knowledge of our own concepts, and scientific knowl-edge where it's relevant. Again, I want to stress the distinc-tion between ignorance and confusion. In his discussion of this, Thomas Nagel says that what we need to solve the mind–body problem, the problem of consciousness, is new concepts. Our concepts aren't good enough. I'm very sceptical about this: that we could solve this problem by introducing some new concepts. And to this extent I agree with the thrust of your question—that what we have to do is get a clear view of the concepts that we already have. This is where we're confused.

NW: *I'm going to press you on the scientific point. If we were looking at the effects of a psychotropic medicine, we could look at scans, we could look at people's behaviour when they take the medicine, we could hypothesize about how it acts on particular receptors in the brain and causes certain sorts of changes in behaviour. Why couldn't there be an analogous investigation that investigates the nature of consciousness?*

TC: I want to say two things about that. First, there is all this evidence from brain scans, and you see pictures in the newspapers: here's the bit of the brain that's responsible for lust and here's the bit of the brain responsible for mathematics. Now for anyone who knows anything about the brain and psychology at all, it's not surprising that there's a bit of your brain that lights up when you talk, and a bit of the brain that lights up when you walk. So this is not a discovery that we should be surprised at. The fundamental puzzle is how it is that anything like this brain can give rise to anything like conscious experience at all.

The second thing I want to say is about consciousness itself. Some neuroscientists have said that we can identify the correlate of conscious experience with some particular kind of brain activity. Now, that presupposes, it seems to me, that there is some one thing which is being correlated with this neural thing. There is something going on in your brain which is correlated with *the* phenomenon of consciousness. And that presupposes that consciousness is one phenomenon. And I'm not sure that we know that consciousness is one phenomenon. For example, when you're dreaming there's a kind of conscious experience going on there that's different from the kind of consciousness that goes on when you're daydreaming. Why should we think that there's one simple quality that associates with all these things that we call conscious experiences? These are the questions that philosophers need to address—questions about the phenomenological structure of consciousness itself. By 'phenomenological'

I mean the structure as it seems to us—phenomenology is the study of appearances. So we ought to study appearances and understand what sort of structure consciousness has from our point of view.

NW: *So in this area of consciousness what's the role of the neuroscientist?*

TC: To understand how the brain works, and more specifically how psychological capacities are realized in the brain, is an enterprise which is deeply involved in philosophy itself. Psychology is very philosophically committed. As soon as psychologists set up a project to understand something like memory, or attention, or perception, they are presupposing certain things about the nature of these phenomena: they are taking a stand on certain philosophical issues. So psychology and philosophy are very closely intertwined. Neuroscientists are further away from philosophy, and for that reason it's harder for the neuroscientist to make a contribution to this problem of consciousness.

NW: *Would it be fair to say that, in your view, a philosopher in an armchair somewhere, thinking, reading, corresponding with people, could actually solve or possibly dissolve the major problem of consciousness; and yet scientists with neurological probes, or with scalpels and their hands bloodied, won't solve it?*

TC: That is my view, at least in the following sense: you don't solve the problem of consciousness by looking into the brain. If I'm right that the questions we're asking about consciousness are the result of confusion rather than ignorance, then the philosopher has to unpick those confusions or unravel them. If we don't believe in a Cartesian soul, or we don't believe there is something apart from the material world, that if we took away the material world there would be nothing left, then what should we think? I don't believe there is a Cartesian soul, so I think that in some way or another we have to find a way of integrating all our knowledge of the material world that removes the mystery that we've been talking about. That's the essence of the problem of consciousness.

16

TIMOTHY WILLIAMSON ON
Vagueness

David Edmonds: *When does a man who's losing his hair become bald? At what hour, or minute, or second, does one become middle-aged? When do a number of grains of sand become a heap? These questions are all linked to a set of paradoxes, known as Sorites paradoxes (the name 'Sorites' is from the Greek word soros, meaning heap). They occur because many concepts, like our concept of a heap, are vague. The very definite Tim Williamson, Professor of Logic at Oxford University, is certainly a leading expert on vagueness.*

Nigel Warburton: *The topic we're focusing on is vagueness, which philosophers have discussed for several thousand years. What is vagueness?*

Timothy Williamson: Vagueness has to do with borderline cases. The word 'red' is vague because for some shades on the spectrum from red to orange it is not clear whether to count them as red or not. Vagueness is not the same thing as uninformativeness or unspecificity, although they are often confused with each other. For example, if you ask me how many people were at a party and I say 'There were at least three people and at most 297', that's a very uninformative answer, but it is scarcely vague because it's pretty clear in what circumstances it is true and in what circumstances it is false. Whereas if I said 'About twenty people were at the party', that's actually more informative because it at least tells you that there were more than ten and fewer than thirty. But it's vague because the word 'about' is vague. If in fact fifteen people were at the party, it's unclear whether I've spoken truly or falsely. So it's that kind of unclarity in the boundaries of what you've said that constitutes vagueness.

NW: *So what's the difference between that and ambiguity?*

TW: A good example of ambiguity is the word 'bank', which can mean financial bank or river bank. But when someone uses the word 'bank' they're using it in one or other of its different senses. That does not imply that they are using it vaguely, simply because it has another irrelevant meaning that you would find listed separately in the dictionary. Not all ambiguity is vagueness, and not all vagueness is ambiguity. The mere fact that the word 'red' neither clearly applies to some shades of colour nor clearly fails to apply, doesn't imply that the word 'red' is ambiguous. That unclarity concerns the sense with which the speaker is currently using the word, not the existence of some other sense.

NW: *Now the classic way that philosophy students meet vagueness is in the paradox known as the Sorites paradox. Could you just outline what a Sorites paradox is and why it's philosophically interesting?*

TW: The classic example of a Sorites paradox, from which the word '*sorites*' derives, is the paradox of the heap. It starts with a thought experiment. Imagine that you have a heap of sand and then you take one grain away from it. Ask yourself whether you still have a heap of sand. The obvious answer seems to be 'Yes'. But the heap just consists of a finite number of grains of sand, say 10,000, so if you keep applying that principle, that if you take a grain away from a heap what's left is still a heap, then eventually you'll be driven to the conclusion that there's still a heap when only two grains are left, then when only one grain is left, and finally when no grains at all are left.

NW: *And why is that a paradox?*

TW: Well, obviously that there's a still a heap when there's only one grain left, or none, is a crazy conclusion. You might think that you can get out of the problem by simply denying the original principle—the principle that when you take a grain away from a heap what's left is still a heap—even though that seemed very plausible when we did the thought experiment. But the problem is that if you deny that principle then, by standard logical reasoning, you are forced to say that there must have been a point when you had a heap and you took a grain away and there was no longer a heap. And the paradox in that is that it seems very hard to accept that just one grain can make a difference between having a heap and not having a heap, given the loose, vague way in which we use the word 'heap'.

NW: *Another similar example often used in this area is baldness. Somebody with a full head of hair isn't bald, but as you gradually lose* *hairs you move towards baldness. Intuitively, there must be a point at which you become bald. Or perhaps there isn't? Could one hair really make a difference?*

TW: In fact this kind of paradox arises for almost all the concepts we use in ordinary thinking. For example, take the concept 'tall'. If somebody is growing millimetre by millimetre, at what point do they become tall? If you are becoming richer, penny by penny, at what point do you become rich? There's just no end to these paradoxes. One can construct them to order, as the ancient Greeks realized.

NW: *So actually vagueness is a concept which is important to us in just about every area of our lives.*

TW: All our language and thought is riddled with vagueness. Although it is always there, most of the time we don't need to think about it—but sometimes it is practically important to do so. We're all familiar with the way in which politicians phrase their promises in vague language so that they can wriggle out of them later. We need to remember the vagueness of their language in order not to be tricked. Sometimes vagueness can have a more positive role. For example, sometimes opponents can end a conflict by deliberately being vague about what exactly they are agreeing on, so that they can both back down a bit without losing face. Problems of vagueness often arise when we have to apply laws or rules or instructions. Suppose that you are trying to apply a law which says that you shouldn't harm your neighbours. You have to think about questions such as 'What degree of loudness of the music you're playing constitutes harming your neighbours?'—and this involves thinking about the vague word 'harm'.

NW: *Is it that our natural language is necessarily imprecise in a number of ways and we should just live with this?*

TW: It's inevitable that our language and the concepts with which we think are, to some extent, vague. We can do *something* about it. For example, when we're framing laws we can make an effort to use more precise language than we ordinarily do, and sometimes we can clarify concepts by defining them. But none of this really eliminates vagueness, because even the language that we use in trying to clarify concepts will itself be vague. For example, if you try to define what it is for somebody to be 'bald' in terms of the number of hairs on their head, then you have to consider questions like how the hairs are arranged on their head, how developed something has to be in order to count as a hair, and so on. So there is never any complete escape. We can reduce vagueness but we can't eliminate it altogether. Anyway, as the example of baldness suggests, it wouldn't always be a good thing to eliminate vagueness because sometimes vague language is much more convenient for us than very precise language. Even the languages of science and mathematics are vague in subtle ways.

NW: *But for a concept like 'tall', you could just say 'I stipulate anybody over 6 feet is tall'.*

TW: Not even that works. For example, you still have to decide whether you're measuring from the top of their hair or the skin, how to deal with people who habitually have bad posture, and so on. There's no end to further questions of that kind. For practical purposes they are ridiculously pedantic, but nevertheless if they're not all answered, then there's still vagueness.

NW: *How, then, do philosophers deal with this problem of vagueness?*

TW: Many philosophers think that what vagueness shows is that the standard principles of logic, as used for example in mathematics, are not applicable to ordinary language and thought. Those principles of logic are based on the idea that when you make a statement it's either true or false, and not both: the principle that there are just those two possibilities is known as 'bivalence'. Many philosophers think that the principle of bivalence doesn't work for vague statements. So if you say that something is a heap, then according to them that need not be either true or false, it might be neither. Perhaps we have to postulate a continuum of degrees of truth between perfect truth and perfect falsity, with all sorts of intermediate degrees in between—that's the starting-point for the approach known as 'fuzzy logic'.

NW: *Do you accept that view?*

TW: No. I hold that the dichotomy of statements into the true and the false applies even to vague language and thought. What philosophers have theorized as cases where something is neither true nor false, or has an intermediate degree of truth, are really cases where it is either true or false but we can't know which.

NW: *So you're saying there is a truth of the matter about whether somebody is bald or not, even though we might not know it?*

TW: That's right, yes.

NW: *What's the argument to support that?*

TW: The basic argument is just some elementary logical reasoning to the conclusion that either someone is bald or they are not bald, because otherwise they are neither bald nor not bald, and so both not bald and not not bald, which is a contradiction. Then, if they are bald, it is true that they are bald, and if they are not bald, it is true that they are not bald, so either way there is a truth of the matter. Obviously we have no idea how to find out which of those two possibilities is the truth. However, the principles of reasoning I've just used there, although accepted in standard logic and in my view fundamental, are not uncontroversial—every fundamental principle gets denied by someone or other. So in order to build a convincing case, one has to look in detail at the alternative proposals that people have made for how to reason with vague words and concepts. What I've argued is that those alternatives do a much worse job than standard logic at handling vagueness and Sorites paradoxes.

Probably the best-known alternative to standard logic is fuzzy logic, which many people have heard of because it is said to be used in the design of some washing-machines and other household appliances. But when you follow out the consequences of fuzzy logic it says some very implausible things. For example, imagine two identical twins, Fred and Ted, who are going bald in exactly the same way. Whenever one loses a hair, so does the other, their scalps are exactly the same shape, and so on. Suppose that we have reached a point when they are both borderline cases of being bald. They are right in the middle: so the fuzzy logician says that it's exactly half true and half false that Fred is bald, and exactly half true and half false that Ted is bald. Then it's an implication of fuzzy logic, given the way the theory works, that it's also half true to say 'Fred is bald and Ted isn't.' But that's a completely false description of the situation, because it's quite clear that if one of them is bald then so too is the other. There is no truth at all to the claim that one of them is bald while the other one isn't.

NW: *So if you take the example of someone who seems to be losing their hair, as our former prime minister Tony Blair seems to be doing at the moment, there's a definite answer as to whether he's bald or not at any moment, even if we can't decide—we don't have full access to the information that would determine that and we don't even know what the criteria are.*

TW: Yes, even if we could be bothered to count the exact number of hairs on Tony Blair's head we still wouldn't necessarily know whether he was bald or not. But either he is or he isn't. Obviously that doesn't mean that it's a fact of any great scientific importance whether he's bald or not. Even if the cut-off point for bald comes with, say, 9,000 hairs, perhaps we could have had a different concept *shbald*, just as useful as the concept *bald*, but with the cut-off point at 9,001 hairs instead. That wouldn't have mattered, but the concept that we actually have draws a line in one place, even if we could equally well have had a different concept that drew a line in a different place.

NW: *So if we adopt your view of baldness the benefit is that we preserve the more valuable conventional logical system where we accept that a statement is either true or false.*

TW: Yes, that's one benefit. It gives an answer to the
question, 'How should we reason with vague concepts and
vague language?' And the answer it gives is one that enables
us to use quite powerful methods of reasoning; whereas
typically the effect of alternative views is that they inhibit
reasoning so that it's difficult to draw any definite conclusions from your premises.

NW: *And is there a wider significance? Could it affect people's daily
lives?*

TW: One sort of effect it might have on people's daily lives
is this. We are constantly encountering situations in which
human beings have to interact with computers, and increasingly we want human beings to be able to speak to computers in their own everyday words, saying what they have to
say in ways that come naturally to them, rather than just
typing in a 'Yes' or a 'No'. If computers are going to be able
to react sensibly to what people say to them, speaking
English or whatever their native language happens to be,
then we have to be able to program computers to handle
vague language. In order to do that we need some kind of
formal understanding of what the principles of reasoning are
that hold for vague language. But my account of vagueness
also changes the way in which we think about our own
knowledge and ignorance. Often we tend to think of our
ignorance as being either accidental or the result of great
scientific mysteries. On the view I'm defending, knowledge
and ignorance are inextricably bound up with each other.
Our ordinary ways of gaining knowledge have intrinsic
limitations. Although there is a logical framework within

which the world has to be seen, we also have to accept that in thinking about the world we can't get very far just by relying on formal rules. There is an ineliminable role for good judgement. But at the same time it would be a mistake to react to that by becoming completely sceptical, because mixed in with all the ignorance there is genuine knowledge as well.

AESTHETICS

17

DEREK MATRAVERS ON
The Definition of Art

David Edmonds: *It used to be so easy. Rembrandt painted art, so did da Vinci, Botticelli, Rubens, Constable, Vermeer. Beautiful paintings were art. No argument. But then came Marcel Duchamp and what he called 'Fountain'—a urinal—a so-called 'ready-made', which appeared in a 1917 show. In more recent times, British artist Tracey Emin exhibited an unmade bed; Damien Hirst immersed a tiger shark in formaldehyde. Are these art? It seems absurd to deny that they are—since they were exchanged for eye-watering sums of money and were displayed in respected art galleries. But, if so, were they art merely because they were somehow linked to the art world—and because the art world deemed them art? Is that good enough? Not according to Derek Matravers, of the Open University—author of* Art and Emotion.

Nigel Warburton: *The topic we're going to focus on is the definition of art. The definition of art has a history—could you give us some background on where the idea of art came from in the first place?*

Derek Matravers: According to the art historian Paul Kristeller, the fine arts as we now know them, which are things like paintings and sculpture and music, were scattered conceptually prior to about the 1740s. So, for example, music was linked to mathematics; others of the fine arts were linked to engineering, or what they would call engineering in those days. Then, in the 1740s, a French thinker called the Abbé Batteaux has this idea that you could group these things together as the fine arts, and that's where we get our modern concept of art from.

NW: *So you're saying one person almost single-handedly invented art?*

DM: Yes, although you need to think about the context at the time. What's recognized as one of the first novels, *Pamela*, by Richardson, had only been published a few years before; the Enlightenment was in full swing, people had more leisure time. It was a period of great conceptual innovation anyway; somebody was going to do it. So it wasn't just a single man sitting in his office, it was part of a larger current.

NW: *Now there are obviously things which we would call art that existed before this time. So what we're saying is conceptually they weren't grouped together beforehand. What was it that allowed this man to group them together? What was the essence of art for him?*

DM: He came up with two things. First he said—and this was probably a mistake—art is the imitation of nature. It was a mistake because there are plenty of things that even he thought of as the fine arts that just don't fit that. But the main idea he had was that these things were a cause of pleasure—they caused in the audience certain mental states which they can enjoy for their own sake. The name he gave to that was pleasure.

NW: *Let's focus on the visual arts, because that's simpler; we can follow them through the twentieth and twenty-first centuries. With the visual arts it's not absurd to think of the eighteenth-century visual arts as being representations which have aesthetic beauty.*

DM: That's right. Beauty comes into it very quickly. For fairly obvious reasons, pleasure turns out to be a rather inadequate characterization of the mental state to which these fine arts give rise. So, we take pleasure in having hot showers and sipping coffee and things like that, and you think that the mental state involved with the arts is more complicated. The German Enlightenment philosopher Immanuel Kant wrote three great books of philosophy. The third book, *The Critique of Judgement*, gave a much more nuanced account of the mental state that arises from our perception of beauty.

So, we have two things here: we have a complicated mental state, which is connected to, but more complex than, pleasure, and a new word—to name those things in the world that cause this mental state, 'beauty'. It wasn't a new word of course, but the link was new. So, beautiful objects were objects that cause this complicated mental state, this aesthetic experience.

NW: *For Kant, there's a strong formal element, in the sense that the pattern of shapes and lines were what determined whether something was beautiful or not.*

DM: That's right. He thought that it's absurd to say 'This is beautiful *for me*'. You can say that you like it, but if you're claiming that an object is beautiful, then what you're doing is asking other people to agree with you. So Kant had this problem. He wanted to say that judgements of beauty were universal: everybody ought to go with them. On the other hand, the account simply in terms of pleasure made them very individual. So what he did, and this is a very simple thought, was to take out of the judgement of beauty anything that might pertain to anybody as an individual and focus on those things which everybody could see in common. He took this to be the object's form. So, he abstracted out colour—because you might prefer red and I might prefer green—he abstracted out everything, except those formal elements in order to get to universal judgements.

NW: *Let's fast-forward to the end of the nineteenth century, beginning of the twentieth century, when there's a strong move in the visual arts towards abstraction: moving away from this idea of representing nature as it is, the emphasis on the brushstrokes, gradually moving towards a total abstraction which didn't relate directly to anything visual in the world. Another aspect of that is Marcel Duchamp's ready-mades, where he found existing objects and placed them in galleries and these were recognized as works of art. How can the traditional aesthetic approach to art, art as beauty, cope with these cases?*

DM: You're quite right, there was a crisis, and it is normally dated to about 1912–14. There are various accounts of what caused this crisis. One of them is that if we go back to the idea of the visual arts representing the world, well lo and behold photography and movies turn up that can represent the world a whole lot better than can painting, so art goes into a crisis. I think an element of that is true, but I don't really believe all of it, for the reason that I don't think that artists prior to 1914 thought of their primary job as representing the world. But certainly there was a break from beauty; so these objects were being included in the world of the arts even though they were not beautiful. The definition of art either had to be abandoned or expanded in order to accommodate these new objects.

NW: *It's almost as if some artists, particularly Duchamp, were deliberately attacking a past conception of what art had been.*

DM: Yes, that's right. The term that described the intellectual current at the time was modernism. Again, like the Enlightenment, there was a huge revolution in thought, and there were huge changes in art as well as in a lot of other things.

NW: *Coming back to the philosophy though, how do we cope with this change? Can we give an adequate definition of art that encompasses both traditional art, visual art of the eighteenth century and afterwards, and the radical new kinds of art of the twentieth and twenty-first centuries?*

DM: Well, a couple of philosophers, Arthur Danto and George Dickie, both of whom were American, came up with a rather neat idea. They claimed that works of art were objects that were linked to a particular social practice. Suppose that you look out at the car park and see two objects: a picture and a Japanese motorbike. They may both be beautiful objects, but what makes the picture a work of art is that it's linked to the art world and the motorbike is not linked to the art world. So these social links came to define art.

NW: *It's important to be clear about what 'the art world' means in this context. It's not just people who happen to work in galleries, who have positions or power in various institutions; for Dickie certainly, it's a much wider category—so that anybody who thinks they're a member of the art world automatically is. Anyone who wants to be an artist is, by that fact, a member of the art world.*

DM: Yes. Different people have different things to say about what exactly they mean by the art world. You're quite right that Dickie's definition was extraordinarily wide. The definition another American philosopher, Jerrold Levinson, comes up with—which is to think of the art world as the historical tradition of making art—is probably a better one to which to link the objects.

NW: *Let's take the example of Duchamp's Fountain—which was a signed, factory-produced urinal. How could that be a work of art? The original has been lost, but Duchamp made some authenticated copies which are now in Tate Modern, the Beaubourg Centre, and various places around the world. How can those be works of art?*

DM: The difference between Duchamp's urinal and a common-or-garden urinal is that Duchamp linked his urinal to the art world, and that's what makes it a work of art. So, to take George Dickie's account of the link, something is a work of art if firstly it's an artefact, and secondly some person or persons acting on behalf of the art world have put it forward as a candidate for appreciation. So what we can see here is Duchamp putting this urinal forward as a candidate for appreciation, and that's what makes this urinal art and the other urinals not art.

NW: *Yet you've got some worries about the institutional theory, at least in the simple terms that we've discussed it.*

DM: Yes. Richard Wollheim, who was a prominent British aesthetician of the last half of the last century, came up with a dilemma for the institutional theory. He said: 'Well, either people have reasons for putting these objects forward as art or they don't. And if they have a reason it's the reasons we should be interested in, because those are what makes the object art. If they don't have reasons, then we have an entirely uninteresting theory because all we would have would be some arbitrary collection of objects.' This dilemma did seem to stymie the institutional theory for a while, and I think it's widely thought to have refuted the theory. But I'm not sure that the dilemma really works.

Go back to one of Dickie's earliest analogies: what is the difference between a married person and an unmarried person? It's not going to be a difference in their physical constitution. What it is, is that one of them has been through a process. And that, says Dickie, is similar to works of art: works of art have been through this kind of institutionalized process. But although it's true that there's no single reason which will explain why everybody who is married is married—people get married for different reasons—it is nonetheless true that for everybody who is married there is *some reason* why they got married. That is what the institutionalists should have said to Wollheim: 'Fine, there's no single reason for putting forward objects as works of art. But for each object, there will be some reason or other why it rather than some other object has been put forward.'

NW: *So you're saying that some ready-made could be selected because it's beautiful or because it seems to be an ironic comment on capitalist society—there could be a range of reasons why any particular work was within a gallery?*

DM: Yes. The good thing about this thought is that you can incorporate all the reasons that existed in the past. You can say Rembrandt's paintings are works of art and the reason that they're works of art is that they're paintings. Duchamp's urinal is a work of art, the reason it's a work of art is because of some mental act or some act of conferral that Duchamp performed. What you're saying is something like this, 'This is a work of art because of *x*', and then you give reasons. Which reasons? Well, whatever reasons happen to be operative in the art world at the time.

So take some of the reasons we have now. It seems to be building on the legacy of Duchamp that there are artists—and I've heard Tracey Emin and Damien Hirst, two modern British artists, say this in interviews—who think that as they're artists, their word is enough to make something a work of art. So you say to them, why is this a work of art? They say, 'I'm an artist and I've just laid hands on this and made it a work of art.' Now that seems to me to be a reason currently operative in the art world, and in my opinion that reason is not defensible. I think that's just a bit of cultural silliness.

NW: *So, you're rejecting this idea of artists having the Midas touch, and what you're replacing it with is a notion that there have to be reasons for choices. There have to be reasons to select one object as a work of art and to reject another. But who's to judge which reasons count?*

DM: That, I think, is the crucial question. Because what we get here is the revenge of Richard Wollheim. Wollheim's initial accusation was that if they adopt one of the forks, the institutional theorists just end up with an arbitrary collection of objects. If they follow my line, they're able to defeat that, but what they end up with is a collection of objects for what I'm sure Wollheim would have said is an arbitrary collection of reasons. Because what still makes such an approach *institutional* is that the collection of reasons that we appeal to are just whichever reasons are currently operative in the art world. I think philosophers should get in there and dispute the reasons that are operative in the art world. The art world gets away with not defending those reasons.

NW: *Do you think that would lead to clearer evaluations of the relative merits of artworks?*

DM: Yes, I think it would. We need to return to a position where people can tell stories about why they're interested in particular works of art that are convincing in the following respect: they will convince people to spend time engaging with them and get some kind of rich experience out of them. For example, I don't know if you have ever settled down to work out how many free Saturdays afternoons you have left in the rest of your life. Once you get to my middle age, it's a really rather small number, an alarmingly small number. Now if we're going to take one of those Saturday afternoons and spend it in an art gallery, then some story needs to be told about why that's a worthwhile use of that time.

18

ALAIN DE BOTTON ON
The Aesthetics of Architecture

David Edmonds: *Alain de Botton wrote three novels before writing a book,* How Proust Can Change Your Life, *which became a bestseller and changed his life. He has since penned several books—all of them international hits. They're both confessional and essayistic. His topics range from literature to travel—and, as we're about to hear, architecture.*

Nigel Warburton: *Wittgenstein was one of the relatively few thinkers who combined a practical interest in architecture—he built a modernist house for his sister in Vienna—with a theoretical interest. He famously said: 'You think philosophy's difficult, but it's nothing compared to the difficulty of being a good architect.' Now you quoted that in your book* The Architecture of Happiness; *is it fair to describe that book as an investigation of the idea encapsulated in Wittgenstein's remark?*

Alain de Botton: Yes partly. And partly it's an attempt to look at the question, what is beautiful in architecture? What is a beautiful building and how do we know when we see one and what's going on when we describe something as beautiful? It falls quite traditionally in a long line of books on aesthetics.

NW: *So what is beauty in architecture?*

AdB: It's many things. When we describe buildings as beautiful we're alluding to material versions of many of the qualities that we think of as good in other parts of life. So there's a real correspondence between what you might broadly call human virtue as listed by, say, Aristotle in his ethics—different qualities that you might find in a good person—and things that are going on in a good building. And you pick this up when people talk about buildings. They'll say, that building looks a bit arrogant, or that building looks heavy, or that building looks elegant. These are words in which you can praise and damn both humans and buildings. My book is an attempt to identify certain themes that are likely to be going on in buildings that are satisfying.

NW: *There's also a sense of the potential moral force of buildings: the way a building might seem to promise to make your life go better.*

AdB: Yes, again this is a traditional question of aesthetics, which is, can good art make us into good people? The hope is also, yes it can. The way I look at it is that works of art do have a moral in the sense that they do have suggestions as to how we might behave. You can look at a glass, a chair, a picture, and it has certain suggestions about what might be appropriate behaviour if we were to take that work of art seriously. But these are merely suggestions rather than binding laws. Good architecture is a suggestion about good behaviour, but nothing more nor less than that.

NW: *It's intriguing for me that you talk about art and architecture interchangeably as though it's obvious that architecture is art. Is that what you believe?*

AdB: The side of architecture that interests me is very close to art and I think it can be called art. There are, of course, other sides. Architecture is also business, it's about shelter, it's about putting your clothes away, it's about lots of things. But insofar as it's been a prestigious and meaningful activity, I think it's because people have seen it in the way in which they've seen many of the art forms.

NW: *But architecture also has a functional element. That became most obvious with modernist architecture. Architects like Le Corbusier argued that the form should follow from the function.*

AdB: That proposal—that form should follow function— has been one of the great red herrings of modernist architecture. Because the function of a building, when we first hear that sentence, seems to be identified with a mechanical side of things, the sheltering side. Whereas, of course, the real function of a building encompasses both sheltering and also what John Ruskin calls 'speaking'. He has a lovely quote when he says buildings shouldn't just shelter us, they should speak to us. He says they should speak to us of all the things that we think are most important and that we need to be reminded of on a daily basis. So the idea is that buildings should be the repositories of certain values, ideas, suggestions, and that they should reflect these back to us, so as to inspire us. That conceptual boldness that Ruskin goes in for gets to the heart of why we really care about buildings in the way that we don't care so much about forks or completely functional—mechanically functional—objects.

NW: *To go back to Le Corbusier, he did talk about 'machines for living'. In his writing he's emphasizing grain silos, ships, constructions where people have been focusing on achieving a certain functional element with a by-product that you get a very streamlined design.*

AdB: People like Corbusier and Mies Van der Rohe found many of the works of technology, in the nineteenth and twentieth centuries, very beautiful. And that's why they liked them. They didn't like them because they were functional, they liked them because they were beautiful. But it didn't fit their agenda to suggest that that was why they liked them. So they appealed to science as the most pres-tigious force in society. If you had intemperate clients and you wanted to try and persuade them that the roof should be one shape rather than another, instead of saying, 'Oh well, I like this shape because it's beautiful', you could say to them, 'Ah no, no, no, it's like this because of science, science dictates it.' That's much more convincing. And we find that same argument going on now with ecological architecture: the same emphasis on the idea that the reason why buildings look a certain way is because the ecological scientific programme is demanding it. If you talk to Norman Foster about why the Reichstag looks the way it does, he won't ever, ever mention the word beauty. But he'll constantly mention air circulation, water pumps, etc., etc. There's almost been a taboo in architecture about the most visceral and interesting

aspect of what architects are up to which is, is it beautiful
or not?

NW: *Yes, in your book you talk about the flat roof of modernism
which scientifically is clearly not a rational way to build. It's sold to the
client as the rational way to build. Actually it's there for reasons of
elegance and beauty.*

AdB: That's right. It's there because, to go back to Ruskin,
it's speaking about the right things. What the architects of
the modernist movement wanted was a stage-set for a
particular way of life that would be democratic, elegant,
based around technology as an almost mystical force for
solving problems. And one could be awestruck—as previ-
ous generations might have been awestruck by the power
of nature—by the power of technology. So it was a roman-
tic attachment to technology. Whether or not it worked
was, I genuinely think, secondary. So even if you look at an
architect like Mies Van der Rohe, many of his skyscrapers,
despite his insistence that he's a builder and he doesn't care
about aesthetics, have all sorts of what you could call 'fake'
detailing. Many of the details around his skyscrapers are
there simply for reasons of aesthetics: they serve absolutely
no mechanical purpose. I don't mind. I think that's great.
All the better for it. But there's an intellectual dishonesty
there.

NW: *If you accept that beauty is a key concept in architecture, it puts
us in a strange position. It invites an aestheticism about living. But
many of us think aestheticism is not the right way to live: we shouldn't
prioritize beauty above certain ethical issues.*

AdB: This has always been a great tension. You find this tension in the history of Christianity—most famously in the battles between the Catholics and the Protestants about what you're going to do with the church. Do you need to spend a lot of money putting angels on the ceiling and gilding pilasters, or can you just get on and worship in a bare room? And you find secular versions of this argument. Should we get on with living, or should we worry about the door-handles? I don't think it's an either–or situation; we're an extremely wealthy civilization and we deserve to get both aspects of life right. Of course, there's such a thing as taking beauty too seriously. Oscar Wilde was helpful in the history of humanity for showing us what can happen when the love of beauty gets out of hand: his claim that he'd be more upset by the wrong kind of wallpaper than a death in the family—it's that kind of extremity that helpfully reminds us that there are all sorts of things that have claims on us: family life, political life, etc., and that a well-ordered life means slotting these things in at the right moment. But to say that beauty has no claim on us is also going too far.

NW: *I was thinking of somebody who hadn't got much money, who's condemned to live in a world of landlord kitsch. Now that person doesn't have an option of beauty.*

AdB: Some people have responded to that problem by thinking, if we say that beauty is very important and there are people who are not enjoying beauty, then that will make that person's life very miserable. And that seems like an unkind thing to do. We must surely focus on the positive. That's one way of interpreting the situation. The other way of interpreting it is to say, if we genuinely think that beauty is important and there are some people who really don't have any access to beauty, rather than denying that this is a problem we should absolutely admit that this is a problem and try and fix it. It's the grossest form of patronization and cruelty to pretend it's not important. You only need to spend time with people whose lives are genuinely materially and practically hard to realize that beauty matters more than ever. And the taste that we would call the chocolate-box taste, the idea of making an interior extremely sweet, very over-decorated, lots of pictures, lots of stuff going on, is frequently associated with people whose lives are very hard. In other words, it's not as though if your life is hard you're happy to be living in a bare concrete cell; you're frequently going to be taking quite extreme and actually quite naive steps to try and improve it and aestheticize it. Think about the garden gnome; the impulses that lead to the garden gnome are very interesting and should not be dismissed. It's the garden gnome itself that should be questioned. It's an impatient response to a genuine desire for sweetness in lives that are very hard.

NW: *So you're not a relativist about beauty. There is an absolute right answer about which things are beautiful and which are not?*

AdB: Again, this is an issue that if forced can tie you up in knots. It's rather like literature. Can we say that the words on the back of the cornflake packet are as good as Shakespeare? I take the common-sense Humean notion, that if people for centuries have seen the value of Shakespeare there's likely to be something in it. We can't say definitively what is beautiful and what is ugly, in the way that we can ask does water boil at this temperature or that temperature. These are not scientific truths, these are humanistic truths. That doesn't mean that they're not valuable truths, because after all we are human beings. So they're part of society's conventions and stock of ideas. It's extreme politeness and scepticism which has led us to a situation where many of the most intelligent and most privileged people in our society will hesitate to say that building Y is better than building Z even if it's utterly obvious. And while they're debating that, property-developers come along and go, 'Oh well, I've heard there's real debate about what's beautiful, and this is our answer and if you don't like it you must be a snob.' This debate has been a gift to property-developers.

NW: *If beauty is in part about the relation between objective qualities in the world and the perceiving person, one way of changing things is not to change the world but to change the perceiver. And it seems to me that what you're doing is trying to move people into a direction where they're prepared to change. You talk about recognizing the aesthetic beauty of a wall of concrete. That's something that's not easy for a lot of people, but with a certain kind of attention it's possible to make a change in one's perceptions.*

AdB: What many writers have done is to try and interest people in things they didn't know they were interested in: to validate areas of curiosity. It's an odd feature about the way human beings work that there are many things that we're interested in that we don't know if it's acceptable to be interested in them. It's one of the minor tragedies of social life that you're often in a group of people and you say, 'God, isn't it amazing the way leaves sway in the wind', and you might be at school or in an unsympathetic area and people go, 'Oh that's pretentious, what nonsense.' One of the great things about life is discovering people who do think that's important and there *is* a weight to be accorded to that experience. And there are other things that we have never really looked at or we have bad associations around. Maybe somebody told us that concrete was nasty stuff that they used in tower blocks in the 1960s and we never went any further with that thought. Somebody else comes along and says, look, something went a little bit wrong, but let's look at concrete, it's an ancient and fascinating material, etc. That gives you licence to develop and deepen that interest. I think that's the role of many, many art forms—to legitimate certain questions and certain sensitivities.

NW: *And if you had to pick out a building that is for you particularly beautiful, which would it be?*

AdB: Well, in London, Tate Modern is an example of a building that does a lot of things well. It reminds us that a good civic building should make a city more liveable, it should be a place of encounter. It's also a building which projects certain ideals. Many buildings traditionally have projected ideals of nobility, the wisdom of ancient Greece and Rome, traditional ideals of classical architecture. Architects have struggled to come up with the idea of what values modern buildings might be proposing. It seems to me that a building like Tate Modern is a quintessentially modern British building. If one asked what would one like life in Britain to be like, I'd answer, I'd like life in Britain to be a bit like Tate Modern, that is, to project qualities of civic-mindedness, of community, a kind of democratic quality and a life that's still quite dignified: the idea that something could be for everybody, but of very high quality. It's a building which interestingly fuses the past and the present; which is something that British life is very cut up and divided about. So that's a building which is not just a good building but it's almost like a good person, a good, modern, British person.

19

BARRY C. SMITH ON
Wine

David Edmonds: *If philosophy drives you to alcohol, don't expect any respite: for booze is no longer a philosophy-free zone. Barry Smith, from the Institute of Philosophy, has come up with a cunning ruse to combine his profession and his passion—philosophy, with wine. Barry has edited a philosophy book on wine,* Questions of Taste. *So what philosophical issues does wine throw up? Here's one. Are there objective standards of wine, or is my opinion just as valid as yours? And here's another, related question: when I drink wine, and savour its look, smell, and taste, am I identifying independent characteristics of the wine—characteristics that I, the taster, am—as it were—discovering in the wine itself? Or is the taste of wine just inside me?*

Nigel Warburton: *There's a story about the philosopher Jean-Paul Sartre, and how he got into phenomenology: he's sitting in a café looking at a glass of water, he says 'Look, I can actually do philosophy about this glass of water in the café.' You've gone one better, you're doing philosophy about a glass of wine. Can you tell me how you got into the philosophy of wine?*

Barry Smith: Yes. Philosophers have always had a lot to say about wine—Plato's book *The Symposium* started with philosophers sitting there using wine to lubricate the talk—but they haven't often thought philosophically about it. And it seemed to me that it was a very good topic. Here's something which we take great pleasure in, something that has a history, and a culture, something which we might think has a value for us in our lives, and yet something which, when we taste it, seems so special and personal and intricate a part of our experience that we wonder if we can share it with other people.

NW: *Well, the first thing I think about wine is taste. How do you get from my personal experience of what wine tastes like to me to something that seems more objective, like a judgement that this particular wine is good?*

BS: Yes, I think taste is a very complicated thing. We talk about taste as something that people can educate, they can learn to be discriminating in their taste—and here we're talking about judgement and refinement, qualities that have to do with sensibility. But taste itself, as a sensation, is something that seems to go on in our mouths, in us, quite literally. It seems to be a very personal experience. How could it be shared with anybody else? The way we bridge those two is by finding another use of the word 'taste'; and when we use it, perhaps we'd best use it in the plural: 'tastes'. I think there are tastes in wine that are different from the sensations we have when tasting it. And I think tastes are things about which we can make judgements; indeed, for which there might even be standard of tastes.

NW: *Can you actually be right about what a wine tastes like?*

BS: The idea that we can't be right and that everything is purely subjective, in the sense of there being only how it appears to me, here and now, is mistaken. We all know that if we've just brushed our teeth, or sucked a lemon, we're not going to get the real taste of this fine Cabernet Sauvignon you've brought me to drink. So we know there are some conditions we have to be in, and the wine has to be in, in order to get things right. That's already a start in getting rid of the idea that there are only just my sensations at a moment.

NW: *So the taste of wine isn't just in the wine: it's about my relationship with the wine, the kind of sensors that I bring to bear on the wine as I put it in my mouth?*

BS: Yes, but there's also a fact about how the wine tastes that might elude you if you're not in the right condition. It might also be that in certain wines, if they're 'closed down', as we say, where they've gone to sleep, you can still taste, if you're an expert taster, that all of the wine's parts are there, and they're just not performing properly. That makes us think that a taste is something out there, something we try to reach for, something we don't always get our tongues on, rather than thinking that taste is just a sensation occurring in us.

NW: *I'm getting a bit confused now: if I had to summarize your view, should I be saying that the taste of wine isn't objectively out there in the wine, nor is it completely subjectively in me?*

BS: Perhaps it's a relationship between the wine and me. But in saying that, that doesn't mean that it's only available to me. If this is a relationship between a wine and certain sensations and experiences I can have, then maybe it will affect other people similarly. Just as we suppose that the colour red is for us a certain experience, a certain way things look, then if we're near enough alike in our colour vision the very same objects will give us the same experiences. So I'm hoping that the very same wines will give you and me the same experiences and these are really shared experiences.

Tasting is actually a very complicated experience. It involves smell, it involves touch—the texture of the wine in your mouth—it involves the taste; and we don't always pay attention to all of the parts of this enormously complex product at once. But if you ask me, did you get the fig, did you taste the pear, I can look back and think, yes, even without taking another sip. I can suddenly realize that the flavours you were talking about were there, but not attended to. So you can bring out, or bring to my attention, aspects of my own experience, that I had briefly overlooked.

NW: *I'm always intrigued with the language that's used by wine-tasters. Some of it seems ordinary language, I can understand when there's a smell of lemon, a citrus smell, that's a smell that I've smelt—so it's actually a reference to something that's in my portfolio of recognizable smells. But some of the language seems to be quite idiosyncratic, almost exclusive to those who speak wine language.*

BS: That may be right. Tasters can be more or less exotic in their uses. Very often they should be sticking to technical terms. How acidic is the wine, what is the tannin like, is it fruit tannin or wood tannin, what is the grain of it? You should be noticing whether the alcohol is hot, particularly at the back of the mouth where alcohol strikes you. But I think sometimes we want to convey more than just a description of the basic elements. We want to, somehow, convey the elegance, the finesse, the harmony, the qualities of overall composition that transform this into a beautifully balanced and pleasurable object. When we reach for those words some bit of the job we're doing is describing and some bit is evaluating. We're trying to describe not just what the properties of the wine are, but also the quality the wine has, as a way of recommending the qualities of the experience you can have in tasting it. Critics, although they often describe tastes as subjective, are in this business of recommending wines to us and trying to tell us, 'If you follow me and follow what I've attended to, what I've seen, you too will have a very hedonic experience, an incredibly intoxicating pleasurable experience.' Partly that's recommendation, and partly that's hoping you'll find what they find in the wine.

NW: *Why should we believe wine experts at all? I know what I like to drink, why should I need advice from an expert?*

BS: Experts have tasted a larger range of wines than we have. They can be our guides to what we might eventually like. But to do that carefully is not to suppose that their taste will replace yours. It's important to find somebody whose tastes coincide more nearly with yours. There will be different populations of tasters, with different preferences, different sensitivities, different attentions to certain flavours, or qualities or compositions of wine. You have to search out the critic who is closest to you, whose passions and reactions, or pleasures, more nearly align with yours, and then you can use them as a very good instrument to go and find the things that might predict the pleasures you could have.

NW: *Wine experts tell us that these amazing, complex, sophisticated wines are the ones with the highest value, these are the things that we ought to like. But what if we just like a cheaper taste?*

BS: I think it was the British wine expert Hugh Johnson who said that he had heard the statement: 'I would always prefer a lesser wine if it had more to say.' We want wines that have something to say, that have a personality. We can have sensations that give us a lot of pleasure, and we can repeat the dose, but eventually we get bored with them. Human beings are such that if you keep giving them the same experience their senses are dulled. They want variation, discrimination, difference. That search for difference, and for rather more complexity and variation, will lead them increasingly on to attend more to what they're drinking and to select better. And the better you select and the more discrimination you exercise, the more pleasure you get in that exercise of that discrimination. That might be what we mean by exercising taste.

NW: *So the role of the expert in wine-tasting is, in part, educational. The expert can open up new experiences for us and tell us that if we approach a certain wine in a certain way, certain experiences are possible. But that presupposes that we're capable of experiencing the same range of tastes as the expert. Surely some people are just better at tasting than others?*

BS: Some people might be better at tasting, though they're not so-called super-tasters. Super-tasters have an intense sensitivity to some taste sensations and may find many wines too acidic or bitter. But I think most of us have got the ability to increase our range, and increase our discrimination, and by doing so increase our pleasure. The more we attend, the more we discriminate, the more we enjoy selecting and noticing differences between wines, the more reward we get from the experience.

NW: *In some areas of life, over-reflection can actually diminish the enjoyment of the activity. So pursuing happiness while thinking about what the nature of happiness is, may actually impair our ability to achieve happiness. Is it the same with drinking? If we start thinking too much about the subtlety of the tastes, and how we're going to describe them, does that deflect away from the enjoyment of wine?*

BS: It would be a danger if we became stamp-collectors and we were simply looking to catalogue wines or classify them, and perhaps even build up blind-tasting abilities to recognize them out of any possible range of wines offered to us. What's important is that in tasting, talking about, and discriminat-ing, we're getting pleasure from wine. And these are pleasures that we want to share—the sharing is probably quite a fundamental part of our nature, and of our being human and social animals. We don't just want to be inter-ested in what the properties of the wine are: it's got to be the experience of drinking the wine that really matters to us.

NW: *There are some very cheap wines around. Some people are happy drinking those. Wine experts tend not to be. Why is that?*

BS: I think it's to do with the complexity of experience you can have. There are some very well-known wines at cheap prices where you can get a simple, pleasurable drink. It might be that you drink because of the pleasure of drinking with other people and because of the intoxicating power of it, but therefore it's the effect of the wine you're interested in, and perhaps the occasion of sharing, rather than the way in which the wine is creating that intoxicating pleasure. A good wine is worthy of more of our effort, more of our time, more of our attention, perhaps more of our money. If it's interesting enough to engage our attention it rewards us by what it can show us, and by what we can learn from it. There are big differences between a wine of £150, which none of us can afford on a regular basis, if at all, and a wine of £2.99. The former is very often more highly priced because it's a hand-made wine involving the skill, tradition and individual labour of people on very exotic plots of land. They're cultivating and creating a beautifully-crafted object which will be unique in history and will last for over twenty or thirty and in rare cases 100 years, and will have a lifetime and a personality and development that outgrows the people who made it. And that will never be the case with a £2.99 wine.

NW: *Some people are quite happy to pay £40 or £50 to watch their football team play on a Saturday—and quite right too, if the team's good. But they would baulk at paying more than £5 or £6 for a bottle of wine. Perhaps wine appreciation is symptomatic of a certain social class.*

BS: Anybody who really loves wine remembers their epiphany. They remember the moment at which they tasted a great wine, a wine of staggering power and beauty, where they learnt for the first time that wine could do this, and they understood that this wasn't the simple drink they had previously experienced. At that moment, they recognize something about themselves and the wine: that a wine can have power and profundity. But also they have the ability to respond to it. What they want is more occasions like this— and of course that's what will lead them on to be collectors seeking out such experiences. I see no reason why somebody shouldn't do that who had previously spent that £40 or £50 watching a football team, who comes to believe that over the couple of hours spent with a friend discussing this wine they were getting just as much, if not more, pleasure.

NW: *I could develop a parallel interest in orange juice. Jaffa oranges have been used for this orange juice, another variety for that one. There are degrees of acidity and textures in different orange juices, and so on. What's special about wine that couldn't be applied to orange juice or ice cream or any range of things?*

BS: When we open a bottle from the cellar that's been there from 1945, picked in the sunshine at the end of the war, we're tasting something that was made by men and women who have long since ceased to live, but who have made this with love and care and who expressed what nature had to offer at that year and that time. They've handed something on to you in which you taste not just the sensations you get, and not just the qualities the wine has, but you're tasting something of history, you're tasting something of their labour and their work, of their traditions and their culture and their settling of that land and soil to make wine for other people to enjoy, to taste, and to learn about. And we can't get that from orange juice.

20

ALEX NEILL ON
The Paradox of Tragedy

David Edmonds: *George Bernard Shaw thought that comedy was light drama in which everyone was married in the last act, while tragedy was heavy drama in which everyone was killed. It's been a puzzle for philosophers for several thousand years that people like to watch tragedies—which evoke feelings of sadness and suffering. The same mystery attaches to horror movies—which aim to shock and scare. Dr Alex Neill has the happiest of roles as the University of Southampton's foremost expert on tragedy.*

Nigel Warburton: *The topic we're going to focus on today is the paradox of tragedy. I wonder if you could begin by saying what this paradox is.*

Alex Neill: The paradox of tragedy is something that philosophers have discussed for thousands of years. It emerges, for example, from some of what Aristotle says in his *Poetics*. Aristotle defines tragedy in terms of the affective, or the emotional, response that it's designed to generate, which is, he says, the *catharsis* of pity and fear. 'Catharsis' is often taken to mean something like a purging or a cleansing of emotion. Whether or not that's right—and there's been a great deal of scholarly debate about the matter—Aristotle makes it clear that he thinks that catharsis, as the end or the *telos* of tragedy, is something that's meant to be pleasurable. Indeed, he says that the job of the tragic poet is to aim at producing in the audience a particular kind of pleasure, and he describes that as the pleasure of pity and fear.

NW: *Okay. But there doesn't sound anything paradoxical about producing pity or fear.*

AN: No, there doesn't sound anything paradoxical just about *producing* pity and fear. The paradox arises when we ask a bit more closely about the nature of pity and fear. That's something that Aristotle himself discusses at some length in another work, a work called the *Rhetoric*. There he defines both pity and fear as painful feelings: pity is a painful feeling derived from the sight of somebody unfairly or unjustly suffering; fear is a kind of pain at the thought of present or possible danger or calamity to oneself or others. So, on the one hand, in the *Poetics* we have Aristotle talking about the pleasure of pity and fear; in the *Rhetoric*, however, he's defined both pity and fear as kinds of pain. So, the idea that the tragic poet should aim at the pleasure of pity and fear turns out to be the thought that the tragic poet should aim at the pleasure of a kind of pain, and there you've got something that looks a bit more paradoxical.

NW: *So the paradox lies in the fact that Aristotle is saying tragedy causes us to feel a certain way. We watch a play, and we feel pleasure. But at the same time, the kinds of emotions that he thinks are particularly associated with tragedy, by their nature, cause us pain.*

AN: That's right. Now, you might wonder whether this is really very paradoxical at all. You might believe that you can in fact feel both pleasure and pain at the same time, and you might think that in fact that's characteristic of our experience of all kinds of art. Where that's most plausible, it's going to be plausible because the pleasure and the pain are directed in different directions. So that at the same time that you're feeling horror, terror, shock, at the content of the story that you're reading or that's being enacted in front of you on the stage, you can be delighted by, impressed by, the artistry with which it's being represented. So as I watch Gloucester having his eyes plucked out, in *King Lear*, that may be revolting; indeed, depending on the nature of the production, it may be physically nauseating. Yet in the moment that I'm nauseated I can be struck, in a way that might naturally be described as pleasurable, by the astonishing way in which the actors up there are combining this magnificent poetic language with something that is so traumatizing.

NW: *I can see also another explanation: that you might be alternating in your response to a play between pain and pleasure. So, in* Macbeth, *you feel the pain as you hear Duncan being gruesomely murdered offstage, and then immediately afterwards you get the pleasure from the light-hearted porter scene, which is a humorous scene.*

AN: I think that's right, too. So we've got two stories now: one is that we might feel pleasure and pain simultaneously, but directed at different sorts of object. The other is that we might feel pleasure and pain in sequence, but now directed at the same kind of object—because in the example you've just given it's the content of the play that is the object of both the pleasure and the pain.

NW: *So, does that mean that there isn't really a paradox of tragedy because there's a way of resolving it quite easily?*

AN: No, I don't think it does, unfortunately; things aren't that easy. Although both of the lines of thought that you and I have been working out are plausible, they don't get to the heart of the problem. Aristotle didn't just say, 'We take pleasure in tragedy'; what he said is that the tragic poet aims to produce the pleasure of *pity and fear*. We're not going to be able to get Aristotle off the hook by appealing to different objects which pity and fear on the one hand and pleasure on the other might have, or by suggesting that we have these different sorts of response, the pleasurable and the painful, sequentially or at different times. Aristotle says it's the pleasure *of* the painful feelings, and that's what's difficult to explain.

NW: *So, do you have an explanation of how you can take pleasure in pity or fear?*

AN: I do have an explanation which I think helps us to resolve the paradox, although it's not an explanation of how we can take pleasure in the experience of pity and fear. I think the answer, to put it very briefly, is that our engagement with tragedy, as a form of art, is not an engagement that can plausibly be characterized primarily in terms of pleasure. I have an explanation of why it is that people for centuries *have* characterized it in these terms. I think it's because for centuries people have recognized that tragedy is a form of art that *matters*, that's especially important to us. And it's patently one that continues to appeal to us; people

stage tragedies and make films of tragedies—think of
modern movie versions of *Macbeth*, of *Hamlet*, and so on:
these things sell. Why is it that people value these works of
art? Well, for centuries people thought that you can only
explain value and motivation in terms of pleasure. That's a
very old theory; you find it very clearly in Hobbes for
example, and in Hume, who says that 'the chief spring and
actuating principle' of the human mind is pleasure and pain.
The thought here is that we're motivated to pursue things
which give us pleasure, and to avoid things which give us
pain. And if you think that our motivations and what we
value are going to be wrapped up together, as surely they
are, then it's natural to think that what we value is going to
be that which gives us pleasure. Given that we patently do
value tragedy then, it must be that we take pleasure in
tragedy. How can this be? And so the paradox gets started.

NW: *From what you've said, you are not completely happy with the
idea that the sole motivation for human action is the pursuit of pleasure.*

AN: No, I'm not. I think that increasingly philosophers have
come to realize the limitations of the idea, although all too
often they haven't carried the lesson over into the philosophy
of art. There are all sorts of examples which suggest that
we're not only motivated to do things because we find them
pleasurable. We can be motivated to do things because we
think we *ought* to do them, because we think it's *good* to do
them, and so on, without deriving any pleasure from that.
The obvious response is that you only do what you think is
your duty, for example, because doing your duty gives you
pleasure, but if you push this far enough back it becomes

very implausible. If I've got a terminal disease and my doctor knows it, I want my doctor to tell me what she knows. And here's my motivation: I regard being in a state where I know that I've got the disease as valuable to me. I think it would just be completely desperate, philosophically, to say: 'Well, if that's the case, it must somehow be that knowing that you've got a terminal disease is pleasurable.'

NW: *Are you suggesting then that a possible motivation for watching a tragedy is not pleasure but the pursuit of truth, maybe truth about the human condition or something like that?*

AN: Yes, I am. I'm not sure that I want to put the motivation baldly in those terms, but I think the reason that we find tragedy valuable as an art form—indeed, a reason why tragedy has often been taken to be a peculiarly philosophical form of art—is that we regard tragedy as a source of *insight*. I don't think we value *King Lear* primarily because it brings us pleasure—although it may do so, not least because of its artistry, its language and poetry. We value it primarily because it directs, with great acuity, a particularly bright searchlight on certain things: Shakespeare says, 'as flies to wanton boys are we to the gods; They kill us for their sport.' You might think that the thought that 'as flies to wanton boys are we to the gods' isn't particularly original, but what is original is the way in which Shakespeare in that play shows us the implications of that thought. I think that's why we value *Lear*.

So I think the paradox of tragedy is to be dissolved in effect by saying Aristotle was wrong. The tragic poet's task is not really to generate in the audience a peculiar species of pleasure. What he should have said, and arguably what he really means, is that a tragic poet aims at giving us a certain kind of insight.

NW: *Horror movies are superficially similar to tragedies in a sense that they invite us to observe often quite gruesome murders or terrible events, and we take some pleasure in them. Do you think the same explanation could hold for those? After all, it's not obvious what insight we get from watching* The Omen *for instance as compared with watching* King Lear.

AN: Yes, I agree entirely. Horror movies look like a problem for me because our experience of them is at least superficially similar to our experience of tragedies. On the one hand, it seems that we take pleasure in horror movies. On the other, we might define horror—indeed, the American philosopher Noël Carroll has defined it in just this way—in terms of its capacity to produce a certain kind of affect: nausea, disgust, fear, and so on. And these are not pleasant emotions. So it looks as though you've got a paradox of horror that exactly echoes the paradox of tragedy, and yet my solution patently won't work. It won't work because, as you've just said, very few horror movies—which is not to say no horror movies, but very few horror movies—can plausibly be thought of as a source of great insight or truth or understanding or anything like that. And it's patently implausible to suggest that people don't enjoy—perfectly straightforwardly enjoy—horror movies.

NW: *So, do you have an explanation of how there could be a difference between these two cases?*

AN: Yes, I do, and I think the difference lies in the kind of affect that's involved, in the kind of emotional response that the two forms of art involve. Tragedy aims at the generation of a kind of affect that is essentially or inherently disturbing or distressing. I don't know if I'd want to go along with Aristotle in defining emotions like pity and fear as kinds of *pain*, exactly, but there's something to that thought. I don't think that the same is true of the kind of emotions that horror movies and novels trade in. Those kinds of emotions are much more like the kinds of emotion that you might experience when you're on a roller-coaster ride. They are kinds of emotions that can indeed be part of a complex of experience that is overwhelmingly negative, but they can just as well be part of a complex of experience that is overwhelmingly, or at least on balance, positive.

NW: *So what you're saying is that horror movies are different from tragedies in that horror movies are more about generating particular kinds of thrill. But couldn't an alternative explanation be that both of these genres are motivated by the dark side of humanity, the fact that most of us, at some level, take a delight in seeing other people suffering?*

AN: You might say that; indeed, people *have* said that about both forms of art. To the extent that that kind of psychoanalytical explanation is plausible, it's much more plausible when it comes to explaining our experience of horror movies than it is when it comes to explaining our experience of works of tragic drama. Even if it's true that we're all at some deep level sadists, capable of taking pleasure in observing the suffering of others, it seems to me that that's just not the best explanation available to us of the kinds of ways in which we value works of tragedy. It's much more plausible to think that it's a decent explanation of the way in which we experience works of horror. Even there, however, I don't think it does the trick. There's a simpler explanation. I think it's just that we are the kind of creature who can take pleasure in experiencing emotions of being thrilled, of being shocked, of being alarmed, of being, in some loose sense of the word anyway, terrified. I suggest that the appeal of roller-coaster rides at fairgrounds is evidence of that.

NW: *How can we tell who's right about this issue?*

AN: One way of telling is by thinking hard about our actual experience of these different kinds of works, our experience of *King Lear* or *Antigone* on the one hand, and our experience of *The Omen* or *The Exorcist* (to take two very different sorts of work) on the other hand. And we need to think hard about the ways in which we do in fact value these works. One way of doing that is by looking at what good critics, be they literary critics or drama critics or movie critics, say about them, at the ways in which they discuss these works when they're trying to explain what makes them valuable. I suggest that if you look at a decent piece of critical writing on a new production of *Lear* or of *Antigone*, you won't find many references to delight, to pleasure, to its being enjoyable, and so on; at any rate, that's unlikely to be the overwhelming theme of the critic's response. On the other hand, if you read a good movie critic on a horror movie, you'll find that there are indeed references to being thrilled or to being delighted as part of the discussion of how horrifying or how scary it is. When good critics write about horror films, the extent to which the films are pleasurable or enjoyable is a major theme; when good critics write about works of tragedy, the extent to which they're pleasurable or enjoyable is typically not a major theme. I take that to be evidence that my explanation has got something going for it.

GOD, ATHEISM, AND THE MEANING OF LIFE

21

DON CUPITT ON
Non-Realism about God

David Edmonds: *Don Cupitt has been described as 'the most radical theologian in the world'. His 1984 BBC television series* The Sea of Faith, *and the book of the same name, gave birth to a movement that is still thriving, and his other books, particularly* Taking Leave of God, *have been both praised and pilloried. Praised by those who see him as making sense of belief in God in the postmodern age; pilloried by religious traditionalists. Central to his controversial views is his non-realism about God.*

Nigel Warburton: *The topic we are going to focus on is non-realism about God. Could you say something about what you mean by non-realism?*

Don Cupitt: Normally non-realism is the view that things don't exist apart from our knowledge of them and the ways in which we describe them: everything takes shape and gets fixed in our conversation. So I am giving up the ideas of a pre-existent self, world, and God, quite apart from human belief, human commitment, and human descriptions. God doesn't exist apart from our faith in him.

NW: *Most people live their lives thinking that there is a world out there that exists independently of their perception of it. Beyond the window out there is a part of Cambridge which I can't see but I am confident exists and will continue to exist after my death—completely independently of me. So would a non-realist say it doesn't exist apart from me?*

DC: No. For ordinary practical, everyday purposes, we can take realism for granted. But remember our knowledge of the world, our vision of the world, and our values are constantly being renegotiated in our conversation, constantly changing. All scientific theory has a limited life, so we shouldn't suppose that the world exists out there permanently and for ever, quite independent of our conversation.

NW: *So my interpretation of what is there is actually part of what makes it be there: the way that I understand the world determines what it really is.*

DC: Yes. I think people are getting familiar with the idea that our whole vision of the world and our values change profoundly from decade to decade. Most people of my age will remember that they have had to reconstruct themselves very considerably during their own lifetime; they don't kill animals with the same lack of compunction as when they were young, and they have different attitudes to women, and perhaps to race as well. We have all had to rethink as the world has changed around us.

NW: *Now, you are famous particularly for having argued that the idea that God exists, as some kind of being out there to be discovered by people, is just wrong.*

DC: That is right, yes. In the traditional popular picture based on the Book of Genesis, God has put us into a fully furnished house, a complete, ready-made world. What is more, remember that in Genesis the first human beings were made as adults, they already somehow had language at the moment of creation and they saw a complete, ready-made world. *Of course* it didn't happen like that! Think how the world must have looked to our ancestors, as they began to emerge from their animal background and become con-scious. By their conversation amongst themselves, they had to learn to structure their experience and build up a picture of the world around them. We have done this for ten thousand years and more, and now we are where we are today. We ourselves had to build up our own picture of the world, by degrees, from within, through our own conversa-tion. That is how the human race came into being.

NW: *Many Christians will say: 'Yes, but God pre-existed humanity and created humanity and we are gradually discovering more about God.' What you seem to be saying is humanity pre-existed God and came to a conception of God. That sounds almost as if God doesn't exist.*

DC: We invented all the theory. *We* gradually built up our own picture of the world, and *we* have also gradually evolved our own religion and our own values. I would say Christian theology was just about right for the historic period between about the first and the seventeenth centuries, during which it flourished. But gradually, as the world has changed in modern times, we have become more aware of our own world-building activity and we have begun to see that we have got to move on. We can't stick for ever with a late medieval world-view.

NW: *You were and continue to be a Christian priest, but what you are saying sounds completely unorthodox.*

DC: Yes, but then Christianity itself has a history. All truth has a history. All truth is developed within the human conversation. Christianity managed to keep up to date until the late seventeenth century, but it has had trouble adapting since then. So now, in a very curious way, you can see Christianity's continuing development better outside the church than within it. The church looks increasingly as if it is falling into the past, trying to keep alive a world-view that the rest of us have now departed from.

NW: *Yet many evangelical Christians, for instance, do believe in the idea of an objective God out there in the world and believe sincerely that there will be an afterlife when they will meet that God.*

DC: Yes, I think you can still maintain belief in God. But remember, since the decline of the old world-view it has becoming increasingly hard to say what we mean by God. I think, myself, that as the philosophy of Plato has gradually lost influence, popular belief in God has got more and more anthropomorphic, as if God were nothing but a very large human being, probably of the male sex (though some would say female).

It is that sort of terribly crude idea of God that I am protesting against. I am saying that our modern critical type of thinking changes everything. By the way, there is one modern version of Christianity, namely the Quakers', that does still exist and flourishes. The Quakers believed from the seventeenth century onwards that we were moving over from the church phase in the history of Christianity to the next epoch, the kingdom phase. God is internalized within each believer: they became a society of friends, not a hierarchical church with sacraments. And the Quakers, of course, contributed enormously to the development of modern ethics.

NW: *Just to get this clear: when we were talking about Platonism, what you mean by that, presumably, is this idea of an abstract 'Form' of God. In Plato the Forms are more real than the phenomenal world that we experience, but they don't exist in the same way that chairs exist.*

DC: Yes. Plato took that strange, hierarchical vision of the universe quite literally—which is a bit of a problem. But it is broadly true that, up till about 1700, when people talked of God they all agreed on what they were talking about, namely a great public object that was the same for everybody, and that God was an infinite, eternal spirit, all-powerful, all-knowing, without any passions, and simple. What has happened is that the popular idea of God has become far too anthropomorphic; it is biblical poetry, but it can't be literal truth—it has lost its philosophical background.

NW: *Yet there is a tradition of a personal God in the New Testament isn't there?*

DC: Yes, but on the whole most of the Bible is too poetic and anthropomorphic in its language about God. We don't know how far all those metaphors can be true. Think of the picture of Jesus Christ seated at the right hand of God. Do you really think you can send up a rocket and find huge, human-looking figures sitting on chairs above the bright blue sky? Of course you don't. We have no longer got a philosophical language in which we can say what is really out there. That is why the old realism has died. We can't imagine, for example, how God can be both personal and absolutely timeless. How can we have a relation with a God who cannot change? When I was young, people really said in response to every personal misfortune: 'Why has God let this happen to me?' I hear less of that nowadays. I don't think people really expect that God will protect them from road accidents or cancer or a plane crash. They accept that life is contingent, there is sudden misfortune. We shouldn't suppose that the whole nature of things is interested only in my well-being—it isn't.

NW: *At one point in your philosophical development you argued that 'God' refers more to human ideals than to anything else.*

DC: Yes, I suggested we should see God as rather like what the Americans call your dream, or your guiding star: the ideal towards which your life is oriented, the ideal you live by. Sometimes I have spoken of God as the pearl of great price (a parable told by Jesus explaining the value of the Kingdom of Heaven). In that case, we might see God as a spiritual goal of life, but not as the ontological foundation of life. Remember, in traditional Christian language God is both our beginning and our end, our alpha and our omega. Now the beginning side, I drop; I don't think we should any longer look to God to explain why there is a world at all, or why the world works in the way it does. But I do think we *can* keep the idea of God as a goal of life: God as a personification, or a symbol, of love, of perfection, of a kind of timeless bliss that we do occasionally glimpse.

NW: *If there isn't a God objectively out there, how can you ground your Christian ethics on anything? Because traditionally, Christian ethics has been based on the guarantee of a real God's existence.*

DC: That is right, and in Catholic theology you should live with a hope of heavenly reward, you expect a pay-off. I say that nowadays everything is contingent and changing; we are transient. We shouldn't expect any external endorsement for our beliefs and values. We have to love them and pursue them for their own sakes. In my own view, the basis of Christian ethics is simply human kindness, kinship: our response to our fellow human being. The world is our conversation amongst ourselves. Everybody has a contribution to make. Everybody must chip in to say their own piece. So for me, just the movement of life is the primary reality, and it is in that that I situate my values. I think, myself, that Jesus was a humanist ethical teacher: he wanted to get rid of the old dependence of ethics on sacred law and tradition and instead to found ethics simply on our response to our fellow human being. And notice Jesus criticizing religious law, when he says, for example, that the Sabbath was made for man, not man for the Sabbath; that is to say, treat religious law purely instrumentally. If it helps you, follow it, if it doesn't, disregard it. He doesn't want us to base our values and our ethics on religious authority. He thinks that is oppressive. Rather, love for our fellow human beings should be the basis of our lives.

For centuries, perhaps for millennia, people have looked for some sort of absolute foundation outside human life, in terms of which knowledge or values or the reality of things could be justified. I think, since the twentieth century, we have come to see that everything is transient; we can't look for any external guarantees for anything in human life. There is only our own commitment to the human enterprise, our love for each other, our keeping of the conversation going. So I believe in jaw-jaw not war-war, in human conversation kept as open as possible as the best way to arrive at a consensus world-view, consensus about truth and a decent consensus about values.

NW: *One charge that can be levelled against that position is that it collapses into a kind of relativism: a moral relativism where every different world-view has equal value and there is no position from which to choose between them. Is that your position?*

DC: No, I hope that our conversation will gradually show that some religions, some values, some works of art, are better than others. There's a useful parallel with art criticism. We now live in a culture which tolerates many different styles in the arts, but we still have art criticism. We can still think that some artists are better than others, and so on. It is true that I am a sort of relativist; but I still believe in conversation as the best way to arrive at a consensus-truth.

NW: *To those who say we don't need conversation because we know the truth—how could you persuade them that they were wrong?*

DC: Well, I would challenge them to defend their views in conversation with me. I hope the mass of the human race won't retreat into various kinds of fundamentalism—I would hate that.

NW: *Many people have said that you are really an atheist in disguise.*

DC: The word 'atheism' has different meanings. Remember the famous line of the nineteenth-century German philosopher Ludwig Andreas von Feuerbach: 'What today is atheism, tomorrow will be religion. What today is religion, tomorrow will be atheism.' That is to say, the way we perceive these terms changes; at one time the Christians themselves were called atheists, because they wouldn't acknowledge the official gods of the Roman Empire. I don't mind people saying my outlook is non-metaphysical. I believe in life, but otherwise I am not metaphysical. I don't think there is anything outside life. Everything is fleeting, including me; all our beliefs are transient. We must simply fight for what we believe to be true and good.

I am not an atheist in the sense of being a dogmatic atheist, because that presupposes that there is one clear fixed notion of God in possession of the field. And that is not quite true: there are many ideas of God current nowadays, some of them better than others.

NW: *We discussed the idea that God might be an ideal we live by, but you've changed your views slightly on that now.*

DC: As I have got older I have become more and more committed to writing books, expressing myself, producing language, mingling with others, getting devoted to my grandchildren, and so on. I now think I love the human enterprise more and more. I am getting more and more sociable. In which case, I am inclined to equate God with life and just commitment to life and enjoyment of life. That to me makes a lot of sense. So, in my recent books, I have pointed to the extraordinary extent to which people have transferred the old talk about God to life. Do you know that near the end of *War and Peace* Leo Tolstoy has Pierre say, 'Life is God, and to love life is to love God'? So that has become a very common idea in modern speech. For example, suppose a young person dies tragically—nowadays, people don't say when they praise her, 'She loved God', they say 'She loved life'. So in my own thought, commitment to co-humanity has become my religion. Perhaps I am now a post-ecclesiastical Christian.

22

JOHN COTTINGHAM ON
The Meaning of Life

David Edmonds: *Today we're discussing a minor, trivial, incon-sequential, topic—the Meaning of Life. It's a subject that threatens to descend into philosophical caricature—the sort that might have been satirized in Monty Python or Douglas Adams. But Professor John Cottingham, of Reading University, thinks that the Meaning of Life is worthy of serious philosophical consideration.*

Nigel Warburton: *I'd like to ask you about a topic that is quite serious for most of us, the meaning of life. What do you think the meaning of life is?*

John Cottingham: Well, I can't give you a quick one-sentence answer on that, but the topic's been very exciting to me, partly because, when I was an undergraduate, we were told philosophy doesn't deal with such questions. One of the exciting things about philosophy today is that it has become a much broader and richer subject than it was when I was a student, and the traditional grand questions are now back on the agenda. There's been a great deal of material published recently on the question of the meaning of life.

The answer to the question is a complicated one. The main problem about human existence is its fragility. The projects that we embark on are constantly in danger of foundering because of the ordinary contingencies of life.

NW: *Do you mean because of death? That's the obvious fragility underlying everything—that we're going to die at some point.*

JC: Exactly, that's the most striking one. But also illness, old age, infirmity. Philosophers have often written as if human beings are grand, autonomous, self-sufficient agents who are somehow in charge of their lives, and then philosophy's job is supposed to be to map out the conditions for the good life. Well, there's nothing wrong with trying to map out the conditions for the good life, but we can never be in complete control of things, because our lives are subject to the kinds of contingencies just mentioned. So a meaningful life has to be one which is not just rich in various ways—a life that includes enriching and valuable activities—but one that somehow comes to terms with this fragility and this contingency.

NW: *So you're saying that as human beings we encounter things, obstacles to our projects. I might want to be an athlete and I break my leg when I'm 21 and it's just not possible. In other words, the contingency that pervades our existence is always liable to upset any mapped-out plan for human life?*

JC: That's exactly right, yes. The other feature of a meaningful life is hard to specify but has to do with the moral dimension. I don't think we can count a life as meaningful if it's entirely occupied with selfish or vicious activities.

We require our lives to have a certain moral resonance in order for them to count as genuinely meaningful. So both these things I've mentioned, the contingency bit and the moral resonance bit, point us away from simplistic answers—for example, utilitarian answers which claim everything boils down to pleasure and satisfaction, or to getting whatever we happen to want—and point us instead towards, to put it loosely, something more spiritual. So questions about the meaning of life are connected with some of the great traditional questions about the place of spirituality in human existence.

NW: *Could you give me an example of a way in which contingencies affect our projects?*

JC: I will, and of ways in which they affect even our moral projects. Consider the case of a dedicated moralist who spends all his life helping others. He decides to build a hospital for lepers, he devotes vast amounts of time and massive resources towards raising money for this project, he works at it, he recruits people to help, but on the day the hospital is due to open it's struck by a meteorite, so his project is in ashes, and he dies full of disappointment and despair. Can we say that he has had a meaningful life? Well, if we define meaningfulness just in terms of engaging with worthwhile moral goals, then perhaps we can. But most people, I suspect, would say that because of the disastrous way this person's plans turned out, they ended in a certain sort of futility. Now you could say with Albert Camus, in his famous *The Myth of Sisyphus*, one of the great icons of twentieth-century existentialist philosophy, that this is just the way things are. We roll the rock up the hill, like Sisyphus. In Greek mythology, he was sentenced to the endless task of pushing a massive boulder uphill, only to see it roll down again each time he gets to the top. He turns around, walks back down the hill, and starts again. Camus says in the last sentence of his essay that we must imagine Sisyphus as being happy. Well perhaps there's irony there—or perhaps there isn't. But it's certainly an absurdist vision. He's saying human life never really succeeds. The rock is always going to roll down the hill. For Camus, we've somehow got to be defiant in the face of that absurdity.

I suppose you could conceivably live that way. You could just say: 'Well, let's just try and live as morally as possible, and when we fail, when contingencies strike, we just walk down the hill and start again.' But that would presuppose a very heroic temperament. I don't believe that you and I could live this way; or perhaps you could, but I certainly couldn't and nor, I suspect, could the vast majority of human beings. We could not live in that utterly heroic way in the face of radical contingency and absurdity. And it's this, the need for some hope that, despite all our weakness, and despite all the contingencies of life and the fragilities of our nature, the good is somehow still worth pursuing and the good cannot finally be defeated—it's this that leads us towards the idea of spirituality.

NW: *So are you saying that, in the absence of hope that humanity will save itself, we have to look outward to God or some other life after death?*

JC: Well perhaps I'm saying that. But I think we should beware of simplistic interpretations of religion which just say:

'Oh well, we can't do it ourselves so it's all going to be fine in the next world.' I'm certainly not advocating that kind of pie-in-the-sky approach. Rather it's this. Simple optimism, that everything will somehow turn out for the best, is hard to warrant, hard to justify rationally. Optimism won't really do. Instead, we need something like the religious virtue of *hope*; and hope and optimism are different. Hope is something which is characteristically a religious virtue. It's one of the three traditional theological virtues: faith, hope, and love. Its cultivation has to do with systematic patterns of spiritual discipline. This is part of the great western tradition of spirituality. We need more than just an unreasonable or jaunty optimism. We need to cultivate in ourselves the moral and spiritual basis for being able to live our lives in the face of seeming absurdity and contingency, and all-too-frequent failure. So that's where the disciplines of spirituality come in. Spirituality is not just a matter of having a metaphysical belief that it's all going to be fine in the next world. One of its crucial elements is the interior cultivation of certain types of virtue.

NW: *And are those virtues reliant on the metaphysical element? Do you have to believe in God to engage in spiritual exercises that could give you the emotional power to carry on in the face of absurdity?*

JC: Well, in a recent book, *The Spiritual Dimension*, and in the more recent *Why Believe?*, I address that question, the relationship between praxis and belief.

NW: *'Praxis' being?*

JC: Praxis is engagement in disciplines and traditions of action and practice, for example, meditation, which are aimed at the cultivation of the virtues we've been talking about, such as hope. Many people think that belief comes first—that in order to embark on a programme of spiritual praxis you've first got to get all your beliefs sorted out. But Blaise Pascal, the great seventeenth-century French philosopher, thought that you should embark on the praxis, or practice, *first*, and the faith would come later. And that seems to me to be the right way round. You can't secure your beliefs in advance, because the sorts of things we're talking about, faith and hope and so on, come as a result of immersion in traditions of spiritual praxis. They come, as it were, after you've embarked on the path, further down the line, rather than being secured in advance.

NW: *If you were advising somebody reading this, what would be the first steps you would recommend they take to find meaning in their life?*

JC: Well, I'm not sure I would presume to advise people in general. There are, no doubt, many paths. I think people do have to reflect on these issues of contingency. They will, in any case, find it hard to avoid doing so if they are reasonably interested in ideas. I'm not saying that only people who are interested in the intellect or ideas can have a decent or worthwhile or meaningful life, but those that are—and that includes a very large number of us in modern, educated western society—must sooner or later reflect seriously on how human life is limited, how many or most of our endeavours are likely to be frustrated in the long run, and on the fact that we're not self-sufficient, wholly autonomous creatures. In a phrase the philosopher Alasdair Macintyre has used recently, we are 'dependent rational animals'. He's talking there about Aristotle's famous definition—'man is a rational animal'—while adding that crucial additional property of being *dependent*.

NW: *Dependent on what?*

JC: Well, we didn't create ourselves. We are dependent on a whole host of conditions that have brought us into existence—whether you believe those are just natural chains of events or whether you believe our existence ultimately depends, as traditional religious views have it, on some divine source. But whichever way you look at it, we are dependent on the causes that brought us into existence. We are also dependent on other people, most strikingly when we are children and later when we become elderly, but, in fact, throughout our lives, in one way or another. We have to live our lives against that backdrop. So part of what I try to do in my book *On the Meaning of Life* is to push against what I think are very arrogant conceptions of humanity, like that of the German philosopher Friedrich Nietzsche, who seems to have thought we could somehow create our own values by grand acts of will. It seems to me obvious that we can't create our own values. We're born into circumstances that we didn't create. We have to find value within a given cosmos, a world that is not of our making. So the first step towards meaningfulness is humility—acknowledging the fact of our dependency.

NW: *I'd like to come back to the practical question, because you're advocating more than a purely intellectual engagement with ideas.*

You're saying philosophy should engage with how you live your life at the level of spiritual exercise. But what does a spiritual exercise actually look like?

JC: Let me give an analogy—that of psychoanalytic praxis. A lot of analytic philosophers are very sceptical about psychoanalysis, and I certainly wouldn't want to defend all the details of Freud's elaborate theories. But one thing that Freudian thought acknowledges is that we are dependent. We don't create our own minds by ourselves; they are shaped and formed long before we become fully rational. Furthermore, we need to understand this and come to terms with it—and the way to do so is through a course of praxis, of guided self-discovery. That, I take to be the psychoanalytic programme. You engage in a regular programme of discussion with an interlocutor. You reflect, with guidance, on your past, and you try to understand yourself better.

Spiritual practice is somewhat similar. Saint Augustine, writing many centuries ago, at the close of the Roman Empire, talked about each person having to descend into the inner self where truth dwells. So religious meditation and the practice involved in that—the spiritual programmes of self-discovery—are not wholly unlike what goes on in psychoanalytic practice. Philosophy too, at least according to the Socratic tradition, is vitally connected with self-awareness and self-knowledge. If we consider the three modes of discourse comprising philosophy, psychoanalysis, and religion, they make up what has often been thought of as a triangle of hostility. Most philosophers are very hostile to psychoanalysis, many religious people are suspicious of psychoanalysis, and indeed many psychoanalytic thinkers are against religion—Freud was notoriously critical of religion. But I think there is a triangle of harmony here. All three modes of discourse, properly understood, are engaged in this deeper, traditional question of self-understanding: the project of linking our theoretical beliefs with understanding who we are and how we should live, if we are to live meaningful lives.

23

STEPHEN LAW ON
The Problem of Evil

David Edmonds: *There is a powerful objection to those, like Christians, Jews, and Muslims, who believe in an all-powerful, all-good God. Stephen Law is here to discuss it. He teaches at the University of London and is the editor of the journal* Think.

Nigel Warburton: *The topic we want to talk about is the Problem of Evil. Can you outline what that is?*

Stephen Law: Well, there are really two problems not one. If we begin with the thought that God is all-powerful, all-good, and indeed all-knowing, the question, then, is *why does evil exist?* or *why does evil exist in quite the quantities that it does?* There are two different problems here. The first is called the logical problem of evil. Some people argue that the existence of God is logically incompatible with the existence of any suffering or evil whatsoever. The other problem of evil is this. If you believe in an all-powerful, all-good God, why is there *quite so much* suffering and evil in the world? Surely an all-powerful, all-good God would have the ability to produce a world with far less suffering, and, if He's all-good, then He would surely want the world to contain far less suffering. Why, then, is there quite so much suffering? So, on the evidential problem of evil, it's the quantity of evil that's really the issue, whereas on the logical problem it's the existence of any evil or any suffering at all that's deemed the problem. The *quantity* of suffering is *evidence* that there is no God.

NW: *So you're treating suffering as evil.*

   SL: Well, it's clearly *an* evil, and it tends to be the evil that gets focused on when people discuss the problem of evil. It might perhaps be better to call the problem of evil the problem of suffering. The word 'evil' comes with a lot of metaphysical baggage. We can drop all of the metaphysical baggage and just talk about suffering. The existence of enormous quantities of suffering clearly is a bit of a problem for anybody who believes in an all-powerful, all-good God.

NW: *Returning to the distinction between a logical problem of evil and an evidential one, do you think they're both equally important to discuss?*

   SL: Well, they're both very interesting problems. I think the really serious problem for theists is the evidential problem. Perhaps the logical problem can be dealt with fairly easily. It would do to show that an all-powerful, all-good God would create some suffering, if that suffering is the price that has to be paid for some greater good that outweighs it. It would be a better world with the suffering in it. That sounds paradoxi-cal, but it's not. For instance, you might say that compassion and sympathy are great virtues and it's important that people have the opportunity to exhibit these virtues, but they're not going to be able to exhibit these virtues unless there are some people who are suffering and for whom we can feel sympathy.

NW: *So that's the logical problem. But the evidential problem is: why is there so much suffering?*

SL: That's right. The issue now is not that suffering is logically incompatible with the existence of an all-powerful, all-good God, but that an all-powerful, all-good God surely would not produce a world with quite so much suffering in it. For me, that argument more or less settles the question of whether or not God exists. It does seem to me that there is overwhelming empirical *evidence* against the existence of an all-powerful, all-good God.

But before we talk about that, it would be helpful if we thought about what makes a belief reasonable, generally. People often get confused about reasonableness and about truth. What I want to stress about reasonableness is that it is a matter of degree. Beliefs can be more or less reasonable. Some beliefs are very reasonable indeed, some a little less reasonable, some not terribly reasonable but not unreasonable, and then some beliefs are highly unreasonable. There is a *scale of reasonableness* on which you can locate beliefs. Take the belief that Japan exists. I've never been there, I've never seen Japan with my own eyes, but it seems to be a very reasonable thing to believe because I've got overwhelming evidence that Japan exists. I've eaten in sushi restaurants; I've met people who claim to have come from Japan; and I've got no reason to think there is some vast international conspiracy to fool westerners into thinking Japan is there when it is not. Having said that, I can't conclusively prove beyond all doubt that Japan exists. Maybe those people who claim to come from Japan spend hours in make-up before I meet them. But still, that Japan exists is a very reasonable thing for me to believe. Other beliefs are a bit less reasonable but still quite reasonable. Is there intelligence on other planets somewhere else in the universe? That's not an unreasonable thing to believe. We know that intelligent life has evolved here. We know there are countless millions of planets like this one; on the other hand, we don't have any great evidence of any such life. Moving down the scale of reasonableness we reach the beliefs that fairies exist, goblins exist, and Elvis Presley is alive and well and living in Swindon. These are beliefs for which there is very little evidence and indeed a great deal of evidence against them, despite what you might read on some Internet sites.

NW: *So we've got this scale of beliefs from the highly plausible to the highly implausible. How does that help us with the problem of whether God exists or not?*

SL: Well, the important issue is not whether or not there is *conclusive proof—proof beyond all doubt*. It may be that we can't conclusively prove beyond all doubt that God exists, and it also may be that we cannot conclusively prove that there is no God. But, even if we can't prove it either way, it might still be possible to establish that belief in God is either very reasonable indeed, despite not being proved, or—and this would be my view—very unreasonable, despite not being disproved. Whether or not we have 'proof' is really not the issue: it's a matter of reasonableness. It certainly won't do for religious people to say: 'Well you can't prove it either way, so it's a faith issue, and *atheism is just as much a faith position as theism.*' That's simply not true. Even if we can't 'prove' it either way, it may well be that the atheist can come up with fantastically good grounds for thinking that there is no God, perhaps as good grounds as for thinking that there are no fairies. After all, I can't conclusively prove that there are no fairies at the bottom of my garden.

NW: *Now, you've said that belief in God is not a reasonable position. Why do you believe that?*

SL: The two things that I would point to are these. First of all, look at many of those popular arguments for the existence of God which non-philosophers consider pretty persuasive—such as arguments about design. Many people say: 'What are the chances of the universe being set up just so, so that there are stable planets and life can evolve? It's astronomically unlikely that that situation should exist by chance. Therefore it is reasonable to believe that there is some sort of intelligence behind the universe.' Perhaps. But one problem with this argument is that it's just an argument for there being some sort of greater intelligence. Maybe it's a good argument. I don't think it is, but let me concede for the sake of argument that it is. What conclusions can we then draw about the personality or the moral character of that intelligence? And the answer is—really none at all. Why conclude that the creator is the Judaeo-Christian God—who is all-powerful and all-good, and supremely benevolent? Why draw that conclusion? We haven't yet been given any reason at all to draw that conclusion. All we have been told, so far, is that there is some sort of intelligence behind things. So that popular argument fails.

So do others, such as crude first-cause cosmological arguments. 'Why is there anything at all? There must be a creator who brought everything into existence!' Alright, there's a creator, but why do you think he's the Judaeo-Christian God? So these arguments are not good arguments for the existence of an all-powerful, all-good God. Worse still, there's fantastically good evidence against the existence of there being any such creator. That evidence is the problem of evil.

NW: *But theists usually have responses to the problem of evil. They've got theories, known as theodicies, which explain how there could be evil in the world.*

SL: Yes. One of the most popular is the free-will explanation of suffering. There are various versions of this. The simplest version says: 'God gave us free will. He didn't make us automata that just do whatever God commands us to do or makes us do, as if we were his puppets dancing on his strings. He cut the strings, set us free, so that we can make our own choices, our own decisions, and act upon them. And unfortunately we sometimes choose to do the wrong thing, and we start wars and steal and so on. Suffering results. But that suffering is outweighed by the good of free will.'

NW: *That argument sounds pretty convincing to me; what's wrong with it?*

SL: Well, one problem is that it fails to explain a very great deal of suffering, such as the suffering produced by, for example, natural disasters. Not very long ago there was an earthquake in Pakistan in which tens of thousands of children were crushed under buildings. They'd just arrived at school, they were trapped underground, dying days or even weeks later in some cases. How do we explain that in a manner consistent with the existence of an all-powerful, all-good God? It won't do to say, 'Well, it had something to do with human free will', because we don't produce earthquakes, not even accidentally. To add to that, let's not forget that it's not just human beings that are caused to suffer in this way. Anyone who's seen the BBC programme *Planet Earth* will know that we share the world with many sentient beings the lives of which are absolutely horrific. Not just now, but it's been that way for hundreds of millions of years. About 250 million years ago there was a mass extinction event—possibly a comet, we don't know exactly—but we know that it wiped 95 per cent of the species from the face of the earth. That would have produced unimaginable suffering. Sharpening up the evidential problem of evil, we can put it like this: an all-powerful, all-good God might put *some* suffering in the world, but he wouldn't put even an ounce of gratuitous, unnecessary suffering into the world, not even an ounce. Now, when I look at those hundreds of millions of years of unimaginable horror, it seems to me that you can't sensibly maintain that there is any such being.

NW: *What you've just said there about hundreds of millions of years of suffering points perhaps not to a good God but to a not very nice God.*

SL: We could consider that as a hypothesis. There is an all-powerful, all-evil God. The first thing you'll notice is that that hypothesis is just as well supported by most of the standard arguments for the existence of God as the good-God hypothesis. If there's a designer, why not an evil designer rather than a good designer? If there's a first cause, why not an evil first cause rather than a good first cause? If I believe in an evil God, I can help myself to those arguments just as effectively as if I believed in a Christian God.

But of course, nobody's going to believe in an evil God. Why not? Well, look out of the window. Right now I can see happy laughing children frolicking around in the sunshine. Why would an evil God allow that kind of thing? Surely a supremely malignant being would be interested in torturing us for all eternity with a red-hot poker, not producing rainbows and laughter and sunshine and ice cream. There's just too much good stuff in the world for this to be plausibly the creation of a supremely powerful, supremely evil being. You can see that this problem—we might call it the problem of good—is just the reverse of the problem of evil. If you believe in an all-powerful, all-good God you have to explain why there's so much bad stuff. If you believe in an all-powerful, all-bad God you have to explain why there's so much good stuff. Actually, it seems to me that you can probably also develop some ingenious arguments to deal with the problem, why does an evil God give us a lovely sunset to enjoy? To make our appreciation of the ghastly dreariness and ugliness of day-to-day life so much more acute. Why does he give us fit and healthy young bodies? Well, he only does so for about ten or fifteen years. Then, slowly and inevitably, people slide into decay and decrepitude until they end up dying, hopelessly ugly, incontinent and smelling of wee, having lived out a short and ultimately meaningless existence. I mean, what better way could there be of maximizing suffering than giving you something good for a short period of time and then slowly and inexorably taking it away? Most of the standard theodicies can be flipped round. And when you flip them round in this way, they're a joke. So, the question is: why do we take the standard theodicies so seriously? On the scale of reasonableness, I place an evil God very low down. But that's exactly the reason why I place the good God very low down on the scale of reasonableness.

NW: *So what is a reasonable thing to believe?*

SL: To get back to the scale of reasonableness, it seems to me that the evil-God and the good-God hypotheses are *both* very low down on the scale. A *slightly* less unreasonable unbelief would be that there is *some* sort of intelligence, only it is neither all-good nor all-evil. Maybe there is a God and he has good days and bad days. If you look at the God of the Old Testament, then pretty obviously that being is not supremely benevolent. He's a rather irascible old sod much of the time, but he has his good days. If you look at the world, it does seem to fit that hypothesis better than either the evil-God hypothesis or the good-God hypothesis. But frankly, we can probably, and should probably, do without any gods at all.

24

KEITH WARD ON
Eastern and Western Idealism

David Edmonds: *Anglo-American philosophy exhibits its disdain for Indian philosophy by more or less ignoring it. But that, says Keith Ward—author of numerous books, including* Concepts of God—*is a big mistake. Take 'idealism'—a theory that the ultimate nature of reality is non-physical. There's a parallel tradition of idealism in both East and West: and according to Professor Ward, each could learn from the other.*

Nigel Warburton: *We are going to focus on idealism East and West. So, what is idealism?*

Keith Ward: Idealism is the view that the fundamental reality is spiritual not material. It contrasts with materialism. If you are a materialist you say ultimately everything is made up of little material bits and laws governing their interaction, so everything is ultimately material. Idealism is the opposite of that: reality is not ultimately material. In fact, matter is an expression or appearance of something which is not material—you could say spiritual, or mental, or conscious. So an idealist would think that ultimately this universe is an expression or manifestation of a conscious or mental reality.

NW: *So this is in the philosophical tradition that distinguishes between appearance and reality. Most of us think we are moving in a material world, while idealists believe that what appears to be just a material world has something beyond it, a deeper reality which is not material.*

KW: That is exactly right. This distinction goes back to Plato: you think you are in the real world of touches and sights and sounds and so on, but actually these are appearances of a deeper reality. Some things in modern physics suggest that might be true as well. Some physicists, those who propound what is called 'M theory', for instance, say that we are really in an eleven-dimensional curved space-time. It doesn't feel like that. And an idealist would agree that reality is not what it seems to be to common sense. Reality, beneath the appearances, is mental or conscious in its nature.

NW: *In eastern philosophy there is a great tradition of this kind of idealism.*

KW: Yes, there is. In fact, it is true of most Indian schools of philosophy that they make a big distinction between matter and spirit. Obviously I am using English words for that (the Sanskrit words are *prakriti* and *purusha*). They say that spirit has a greater reality than matter. There are lots of different Indian schools of philosophy, but most people would say that the dominant one is Vedanta, a philosophy that is based on the Indian sacred scriptures, the *Upanishads*. Vedantic schools are idealist, basically, and they say that Brahman—you could translate that as the Absolute Reality—has the nature of being, consciousness, and bliss, *Sat—Chit—Ananda*, and everything is part of that one underlying reality. That's the Vedantic school of philosophy, which is one of the six major Indian schools of philosophy, and, as I say, probably the best-known among philosophers.

NW: *So that combines idealism with a kind of monism—everything is ultimately one underneath the world of appearances.*

KW: That is right. An idealist does not have to be a monist. You could think, like the English philosopher John McTaggart, that there are lots of different minds. Jains, the Indian-originated religious group, believe that too. But the Vedantic tradition is monistic. They would use a text from the *Upanishads* to support their position that 'all is Brahman'—everything is one—we are all parts of this absolute reality.

NW: *What follows from that belief in the Vedantic tradition? How should we live? How should we interact with the material world?*

KW: Well, there are different interpretations, as always. But one interpretation would be that you and I aren't really different beings. We are not alien to each other; we are, literally, part of the same united reality. The claim would be that to see that, you would probably have to be enlightened; and if you were enlightened and you saw that we are all parts of one reality, then that would overcome opposition and conflict and violence, because you would think, 'nothing is mine and nothing belongs to me, because I am just part of the whole'. So there is an ethical implication of this, for most Vedantians. I suppose the view would be that our individual selves are illusory in some sense: they are like the skins of an onion, you peel them away, your personality, your traits, different dispositions you have. You take those away and you find that your true self, which is called *Atman*, the true inner self, is actually the same in everyone. We literally aren't different, in some sense. Separateness and individuality is an illusion, an illusion due to ignorance. When you realize that you are not an individual self that can possess something, but you are actually identical in your innermost reality with everyone else and with everything else, then possessiveness becomes a logical absurdity. That is the claim of one of the greatest Vedantin philosophers, probably the best-known in the West, Shankara, who lived probably in the eighth century AD.

NW: *Was he a Buddhist philosopher?*

KW: That is a very good question. Absolutely not, but yes! By that I mean his philosophy was invented in order to get rid of Buddhism from India, which he successfully accomplished. But he did it by taking over all the Buddhist insights. This is a very naughty thing to say, but most scholars would agree that what Shankara did was use all the Buddhist insights, incorporate them into Hinduism, and say, 'we don't need Buddhism any more because we have got it all'. So he is *crypto*-Buddhist. But he would definitely say: 'I am absolutely not a Buddhist!'

NW: *Now, to be a bit sceptical here, why would anybody believe this—what is the evidence?*

KW: That is not a question that would have arisen for Shankara or for the other best-known Vedantin philosopher

Ramanuja. They believed in scriptural authority. If you look
at classical Indian philosophy in the early medieval period,
they just accept the *Upanishads* and the *Veda* as revealed,
divinely given truth—given by the gods or supernatural
beings. So Shankara just said: 'I believe this because it is in
the scriptures.' Now things have changed, interestingly. So if
you go to India today and you look at Vedantin philosophers,
they will say, 'the evidence is personal experience of liberation'; so you know that it is true because you meditate, you
break through the boundaries of self and egoism, and you
actually experience a unity with the all. That stress on
experience, ironically, comes from the German philosophical
tradition which has been imported into India since the
nineteenth century and has given rise to what is now called
Neo-Vedanta. Neo-Vedanta doesn't say, 'we believe this just
because it is in the scripture'. Neo-Vendantins would say, 'we
believe this because somebody, perhaps me but perhaps some
guru that I follow, has experienced liberation and experienced this unity with the all'. So now it is personal experience that has become important. That is not true for the
classical tradition.

NW: *Obviously within the western philosophical tradition idealism is
associated with German eighteenth- to nineteenth-century philosophy. Is
there a causal influence there? Does German philosophy borrow from
Indian idealism?*

KW: Many PhDs have been written on this subject. My
own view is that there wasn't a close textual influence.
People like Hegel in Germany had not carefully read all the
Indian philosophers. They didn't have the languages and

they didn't have access to the scriptures, as we now do, thanks to the Internet and so on. So they didn't have the knowledge; but they got some big ideas, I think, from India. Hegel's big idea can be centred on his definition of infinity. Classically Christian philosophers in the West had said that God is infinite and the infinite is completely opposed to the finite, and therefore God, the infinite, and the finite universe have nothing in common. They are completely different; the infinite excludes the finite by definition. What Hegel did was to say, 'no, actually the concept of infinity entails that nothing is outside it. If it is infinite it excludes nothing. Therefore, by definition, but a different definition, everything must be part of the infinite'; and that was the big move Hegel made to a monistic and spiritual view of what he called the ultimate reality, *Geist* or absolute spirit. This move originated in Hegel thinking about what was meant by the notion of infinity—which was becoming a subject of enquiry in mathematics as well at that time. That debate wasn't influenced by the Indian traditions, but Hegel had read the available texts, the *Upanishads* and so on, and must have seen a similarity. So there was a general influence, but it wasn't technically informed—and Hegel, I am sorry to say, didn't think much of Indian religious thought.

NW: *But Schopenhauer was more explicitly indebted to Indian thought, I believe.*

KW: He certainly was. But again he didn't really know the texts in any detail. He knew what had been translated of the *Upanishads*; and of course they are partly, but importantly, philosophical documents. If you read the Bible it is not philosophical, you would find it very difficult to find philosophical arguments in it; but in the *Upanishads* you find a concentration on the nature of reality, the nature of the self, and the argument that the true self is identical with the supreme reality.

So they are partly philosophical sorts of texts, and Schopenhauer was very influenced by them. One reason they were used by Schopenhauer in particular was because he didn't like the very anthropomorphic views of God with which he was familiar in German Lutheranism. He thought, you've got to get away from thinking of God as a person who arbitrarily sends people to hell or not. So I think he found in the Indian tradition a very different approach; though still a spiritual approach. Schopenhauer, although he was called the first great German atheist, wasn't really an atheist at all: he just didn't like God. He didn't like the word 'God'. But he thought that the nature of reality was spiritual. He was an idealist, in other words, and I think, yes, he was really influenced by Indian modes of thought.

NW: *In Anglo-American philosophy, idealism flourished at the end of the nineteenth century. But now most contemporary British and American philosophers look on that as a phase that we have moved beyond. Is that a fair assessment?*

KW: I think that is a fair assessment of the actual situation, but there are a few of us idealists left, and we are a growing band; there will be four by next year! Idealism is not fashionable—that is very true. One reason for that is the great success of science which focuses on explaining human, mental elements of consciousness in neuro-physiological terms. That's had a great influence towards materialism. But I think most of the main arguments for idealism are still in place, and quite surprisingly perhaps you can find them in the work of some quantum physicists. People like Roger Penrose, the Oxford mathematical physicist, for example. He says that maybe consciousness is fundamental to reality, in some sense. And some mathematicians and physicists, as well as a number of philosophers, are prepared to 'come out' as Platonists—so there are a few of us.

The big question still remains, isn't it true that consciousness may have an ineliminable place in our ontology? You can't get rid of it. And then the question is, well does it just emerge from matter? If it is different from matter, does it just emerge? Or could matter be seen as something which only exists when consciousness exists? That is a view I would hold myself. Obviously I'd need a long time to convince anybody, if I ever could, but idealism is still around in that form. All the things we see and touch and feel are actually elements of consciousness. Possibilities collapse into actualities only in consciousness—and maybe possibilities can only exist in consciousness too. That is a philosophical view that is still worthy of careful examination.

NW: *In your own philosophical development have you felt that you have learnt from your studies of Indian philosophy anything that you couldn't have learnt from the study of western philosophy?*

KW: Well, I think the Indian philosophical traditions are very interesting. They begin from a different place than the western tradition. The western tradition begins from thinking that a supreme consciousness would be a creator who is not identical with the creation and who created, for some reason, to get something done of some sort. Whereas Indian traditions don't start there; they start from asking, what is the nature of *this* reality that we are in? They say, in the Vendantic tradition, that its nature is pure spirit. So they are not talking about another reality, they are talking about the true inner nature of this reality. There is no reason why Indian idealists shouldn't talk about God; they usually do, in fact, say that God is a sort of picture image of absolute consciousness. But you mustn't think of God as another person. That would be quite wrong.

This is a philosophically deep view. You are asking questions about the nature of consciousness and whether consciousness is necessarily something that has to be embodied in a human brain and body. My own answer, is 'no, not necessarily'. I don't see any necessity in that. And then if you explore the hypothesis that there is a consciousness which isn't at all embodied and which could have something like thoughts and intelligence, then it would be possible that this material universe was an expression of that cosmic consciousness. You could then go on to see whether the observed facts are illuminated by such a hypothesis. I think they are.

Perhaps I should say that in the Indian tradition there are two ways of taking this postulate of the material world as the expression of a supreme spiritual reality, which you might call a negative way and a positive way. The negative way is, you say 'the whole of our empirical reality is an illusion'. People use the word *Maya*. An illusion is something that is simply false; it is like a mirage in the desert, and you say, 'well, it is not there'. Once you see through it, you see that reality is just the one unified consciousness. That is the negative view. But there is a positive view which is more associated with Ramanuja rather than Shankara.

Ramanuja probably lived in the twelfth century AD. He came after Shankara, and he held that the material universe is not an illusion. The model that Ramanuja used was that the world, the universe, is the body of the lord. So the idea of the universe as God's body actually goes back to twelfth-century Indian philosophy. Saying that the world is the body of God has a positive feel; for then maybe the universe is an expression of some of the potentialities within the divine consciousness which have to be expressed.

That sounds very much like Hegel—that the whole of history is the progressive self-revelation of the absolute spirit. Where Hegel introduced something new was the idea of evolution or development—that history is a progressive revelation of the absolute. This passed back into more recent Indian thought which is able to accept an evolutionary view in the sense of a progressive revelation, bit by bit, of what absolute reality is like.

NW: *Given the richness of the philosophical tradition in Indian thought, why do you think it has been so marginalized in western philosophy departments?*

KW: Well, the language is difficult: you have to have Sanskrit, and Sanskrit is a very difficult language to learn. And it is partly because the Indian traditions are classically scripturally based on a very different scripture—the *Upanishads*—from anything in the West. Western philosophers have tended to say, 'this is not philosophy, this is just taken from an allegedly revealed knowledge'. But you have to take your premises from somewhere anyway, and the interesting philosophical question is, where do we go from there? Perhaps, as I have suggested, there may also be independent arguments for idealism—arguments from consciousness and personal experience—that are worth exploring. It's a pity, however, that both Indian philosophy and idealism are rather neglected fields in the West. Maybe this will all change, as the pendulum swings again, as it so often does in the history of philosophy.

25

A. C. GRAYLING ON
Atheism

David Edmonds: *Professor A. C. Grayling is an author so prolific that the suspicion in the philosophy world is that he runs a secret team of underlings, churning out essays, reviews, and books on his behalf. Never one to duck controversy, he's a prominent public intellectual, commenting as a philosopher on an extensive range of issues. A recent book is entitled* Against All Gods. *That gives a subtle clue to his uncompromising stance on religion.*

Nigel Warburton: *We're focusing on 'atheism' for this discussion: what do you understand by that term?*

A. C. Grayling: Atheism is a rejection of the idea that there are gods or supernatural agencies of any kind in the world. It is even a rejection of the idea that there *might* have been supernatural agencies at some earlier point in the universe's history, which is the deist position. I am an atheist, but I don't like the term very much. I don't like it for this reason: it makes matters look as though there is something worth denying the existence of. I much prefer the term *naturalist*, to mean somebody who thinks that the universe is a realm of

natural law: one where the concepts of physics and chemistry
describe what there fundamentally is in this universe of ours,
without need or indeed room for a supernaturalistic or
magical supplement. It does not say that all phenomena—
such as the human need for poetry and beauty—are reduc-
tively explicable by, say, the chemistry of the nervous system.
There are naturally emergent properties of complex systems
which enter into an account of the intentional and social
aspects of reality as it most interests creatures like us. But it
does say that, ultimately, whatever there is, is part of nature
and arises from it.

NW: *Is that consistent with agnosticism?*

ACG: Agnosticism is the view that you don't know whether
or not there are supernatural agencies, and it seems to me a
wishy-washy, fence-sitting kind of view. The question at
stake here is about rationality. The intellectual respectability
of the claim that there are gods, say the gods of Olympus or
the gods of Hinduism, or one god, say the God of Judaism,
seems to me exactly on a par with the intellectual respectability of thinking there are fairies at the bottom of your
garden. Belief in fairies was very widespread until the late
nineteenth century: indeed, people believed that fairies were
far more present in their lives than God was. Things that
went missing, for example, such as shoelaces or teaspoons,
had been stolen by fairies, they thought. So the comparison
here is not a joke one. And if you think that the reasons you
have for believing there are fairies are poor reasons, and that
it's irrational to think that there are such beings, then belief
in supernatural agencies in general is irrational in the same

way. So for me it's a question of the rationality of belief. Agnostics, who think there is as much chance that there might be such entities as that there might not be such entities, fall foul of these strictures. There is no fifty–fifty likelihood about the existence of fairies—or other putative supernatural entities.

NW: *One argument that religious believers quite often use is that the world has been so perfectly designed that there must have been a God to do it. This approach has had a new lease of life with so-called Intelligent Design. Do you have a view on that?*

ACG: Yes I do. The Intelligent Design movement is a fig-leaf, a big one, for creationism. What its proponents wish to do is to promote the intelligibility and also the rationality of the idea that there might be a conscious purpose behind the way things are in the universe. Yet we have an extremely powerful and very deep theory about how appearance of design and organization in the universe emerges, not least in the biological realm, in the form of Darwinian theory. If you took seriously the thought that there is or was a designer, that designer would have to be a particularly incompetent one, because there are so many ways in which the universe could be very much better organized than it is: the human body, for example, has a few bad design features of an almost actionable kind—one would have a case in law against the designer, if there were one!

NW: *But there's a response that believers give there, which is that God moves in mysterious ways.*

ACG: It's such an easy one, that one; it gets you out of all sorts of holes. In fact that leads on to this rather interesting thought. If you invoke the notion of an omniscient, omnipotent, eternal being, the standard idea of God, absolutely anything follows, and correlatively nothing counts as counter-evidence against the existence of a God. We're all familiar with Karl Popper's dictum that if a theory or claim purports to explain everything, and nothing counts as inconsistent with the claim, then it's empty: it explains nothing and does no work.

NW: *Opponents of that kind of view will say: 'That's not that dissimilar to science. Science actually purports to explain everything and everything which it hasn't yet explained will at some future date be explicable by that method.'*

ACG: I don't think science claims that at all. Science at its best is a public, testable, challengeable project, always having to maintain its own respectability by saying what would serve as counter-evidence against its hypotheses and concepts. When people put forward views in science they publish them so that other people can test them, review them, try to replicate results, and I think that is absolutely the model of how epistemology should proceed: out there in the open, and inviting the very toughest kind of response from other people. Now of course what science premises, extra-theoretically, is the idea that the universe is a place that can be understood: that it's a fundamentally intelligible realm, that if we have got the right concepts, the right procedures, and the right instruments, we will be able to increase our understanding of it and maybe, in the ideal, come to a full understanding of it. But that is a kind of methodological ideal: there's going to be plenty of work for scientists in their pursuit of achieving that.

NW: *I find myself in the slightly strange position here of playing God's advocate. Carrying on in that vein, couldn't you say that there would be no morality without God?*

ACG: That is an old canard. It entirely ignores the fact that in the classical tradition of antiquity there are deep, rich, powerful thoughts about the foundations of ethics and the nature of the good life which make no appeal whatever to any divine command or any government by a spirit-monarch in the sky who will reward you if you do what he or she requires and punish you if you don't. All the very best and deepest thinking about ethics has come from non-religious traditions. To suggest that it's not possible to have an ethics unless you think there is a rewarder and punisher up there in the sky, that you need an enforcer for morality, is a calumny on all those whose reasons for behaving as they do towards others—their desire to respect others, to try to be collegial, to foster the project of cooperation in society—is premised solely on their liking for and sympathies for their fellow human beings, grounded on their reflection on human nature and the human condition, and the question of what is good. And by the way, there's a logical fallacy involved in the idea that morality needs an enforcer, that you do something because somebody will beat you up if you don't: the fallacy of *argumentum ad baculum* (also known as the 'appeal to force', the argument where force or the threat of force is given as a justification for a conclusion). Indeed, people whose morality comes in a box that they've taken off a shelf in the supermarket of ideas—marked 'Catholicism' or 'Islam' or such—are much less honourable and admirable than those who've thought for themselves about these things.

NW: *As an atheist, you're not obliged to believe that death is final, but actually most atheists do believe that. Where do you stand on that issue?*

ACG: I think death is, gratefully, final. It's no different from the state that we were in before we were conceived. Even though life is very short—I'm fond of pointing out to people that the average human life is less than 1,000 months long, which is a good reason for not wasting time if one can help it—that fact provides a definite and useful *terminus ad quem*. It means that the things that you want to achieve must be achieved here. You must work: 'work while you have light', as the nineteenth-century Swiss philosopher Henri-Frédéric Amiel said. But it also means that in the end there will be a wonderful rest from it all. You will survive in the way science tells us, which is that our constituents return to the elements, and become part of nature, and remain permanently part of nature, because that, after all, is what the conservation-of-energy law tells us. We're not going to disappear entirely—in the form of the bits that we're made of.

NW: *The reasons that you gave would make death being final a good thing. But they're not reasons for believing that death is final.*

ACG: There's no evidence of any convincing kind, apart from anecdotal tales about ghosts, which suggests that there is any form of continued existence following death. I'd be interested to hear what would count as such evidence. I've had the experience of meeting people who are terrified by the thought that there is an alternative dispensation, or that they might remain conscious in some way after death, locked in a coffin or sliding into the furnace or meeting beings on the other side of the Styx, being a new boy all over again in a new world: in prospect it seems rather exhausting, as well as silly.

NW: *Many millions of people around the world do believe in God or gods. They seem to get quite a lot out of it. Do you begrudge them that?*

ACG: Yes and no—which is a good philosophical answer! I understand why it is that people might find comfort or solace in having something to hang on to in times of distress. It would be cruel on an occasion when somebody has that deep need to say: 'What you believe is a load of rubbish.' I also recognize that the church in its heyday, when it was wealthy and could commission lots of works of art and oratorios, gave plenty of work to artists, some of whom were sincere in their work and some of whom doubtless laughed all the way to the bank. So in different ways, both on the personal front and the public front, the phenomenon of belief was not always or wholly bad. But, on the other hand, the record of organized religion in human history has been a dismal one, and on balance far more negative than positive. It's been the source of tremendous conflict and tremendous oppression. It has been so both internally, from the point of view of individuals agonizing over such matters as sexuality and sin, and externally in dividing people from one another and providing reasons for them to murder one another. It has been an oppressive burden in human history, even though it paid for the Sistine Chapel and helped people on their own, frightened at night, to feel a little safer.

NW: *I've been struck by how, recently, there's been a glut of books about atheism by, amongst others, Daniel Dennett, Richard Dawkins, and Julian Baggini. Do you think we're in a golden age of atheism right now?*

ACG: I don't know about that. I think those books are a reaction to what looks like a resurgence of religion in our contemporary world. I don't myself think that we're seeing a resurgence of religion; I think we're seeing a mighty turning-up of the volume by the religious, which is a different thing. That might well be a symptom of the fact that religion feels so under pressure that it's doing what it did in the sixteenth century, at the time of the Reformation, when Catholicism, which had been the single dominant outlook in western Christendom, became vigorous in trying, unsuccessfully, to recover its lost hegemony over the mind of Europe. These were death-throes that caused the awful wars of the sixteenth and seventeenth centuries, wars caused by the church's loss of power and the futile but murderous struggle to regain it. It might well be that—with globaliza-tion and the fact that Islamic culture, in particular, feels greatly under pressure and threatened by the rapid spread of what must seem unacceptable aspects of western morality—it is a case of irritation, anxiety, and frustration being ratcheted up.

So in response to the religious amplifiers being turned up, of course people have been arguing against the religious noise. And on the following two grounds: first, the irration-ality of religious belief itself; and secondly, the crucial question of the place of religion in public debate—that is, in the public domain and in politics. What one doesn't want to see is a relatively small group of people imposing traditional-ist and often reactionary views on everyone else. Remember that in the UK the people who go every week to mosque, temple, synagogue, or church constitute about 8 per cent of the population. And yet they're given a huge amount of air-time on the BBC, they get public tax money for their faith-based schools, they've been arguing for exemption from various anti-discrimination laws. These things are unacceptable. So there's a very serious debate to be had here about the place of religion in the public domain, given that our culture is a functionally secular one. Secularism is something that religions themselves should be embracing for their own survival. Because if any one religion were to become dominant in the public sphere, the inevitable result is that the other ones will be marginalized or even eventually silenced. So it would do all of us good if a secular dispensation were to persist, having been won with such difficulty in the last few centuries.

NOTES ON CONTRIBUTORS

David Edmonds is a research associate at the Oxford Uehiro Centre for Practical Ethics, a radio documentary maker for the BBC World Service, and a contributing editor of *Prospect* Magazine.

Nigel Warburton is Senior Lecturer in Philosophy at the Open University, an Honorary Research Fellow at the Institute of Philosophy, University of London, and a Fellow of the Royal Society of Arts.

Julian Savulescu holds the Uehiro Chair in Practical Ethics at the University of Oxford, and is Director of the Oxford Uehiro Centre for Practical Ethics.

Simon Blackburn is Professor of Philosophy at the University of Cambridge, and a Fellow of Trinity College Cambridge.

Peter Singer is the Ira W. DeCamp Professor of Bioethics in the University Centre for Human Values, Princeton University, and Laureate Professor at the Centre for Applied Philosophy and Public Ethics at the University of Melbourne.

Michael Sandel is the Anne T. and Robert M. Bass Professor of Government Theory in the Department of Government at Harvard University.

Alexander Nehamas is Edmund Carpenter II Class of 1943 Professor in the Humanities, in the Philosophy Department of Princeton University.

Kwame Anthony Appiah is Laurance S. Rockefeller University Professor of Philosophy at the Centre for Human Values, Princeton University.

Miranda Fricker is Reader in Philosophy at Birkbeck, University of London.

Anne Phillips is Professor of Political and Gender Theory in the London School of Economics Gender Institute and Government Department.

Will Kymlicka holds the Canada Research Chair in Political Philosophy in the Philosophy Department of Queen's University, Kingston, in Canada.

Wendy Brown is Professor of Political Science at the University of California, Berkeley.

A. W. Moore is Professor of Philosophy at the University of Oxford and Tutorial Fellow of St Hugh's College, Oxford.

David Papineau is Professor of Philosophy at King's College London.

Barry Stroud is the Willis S. and Marion Slusser Professor of Philosophy at the University of California, Berkeley.

Hugh Mellor is Emeritus Professor of Philosophy in the Faculty of Philosophy, University of Cambridge.

Tim Crane is Knightbridge Professor in Philosophy at the University of Cambridge.

Timothy Williamson is Wykeham Professor of Logic at the University of Oxford and a Fellow of New College, Oxford.

Derek Matravers is Senior Lecturer in Philosophy at the Open University.

Alain de Botton is a writer and broadcaster.

Barry C. Smith is Professor of Philosophy at Birkbeck, University of London, and Director of the Institute of Philosophy.

Alex Neill is Reader in Philosophy at the University of Southampton.

Don Cupitt is a Life Fellow of Emmanuel College, Cambridge.

John Cottingham is a Professor Emeritus of Philosophy at Reading University and an Honorary Fellow of St John's College, Oxford.

Stephen Law is Senior Lecturer in Philosophy at Heythrop College, University of London. He is also a Fellow of the Royal Society of Arts.

Keith Ward is Regius Professor of Divinity Emeritus at Oxford University.

A. C. Grayling is Professor of Philosophy at Birkbeck, University of London, and a Supernumerary Fellow of St Anne's College, Oxford. He is also a Fellow of the Royal Society of Arts.

FURTHER READING

CHAPTER 1

Julian Savulescu and Nick Bostrom (eds.), *Human Enhancement* (Oxford: Oxford University Press, 2009).

Helga Kuhse and Peter Singer (eds.), *A Companion to Bioethics* (Oxford: Blackwell, 1998).

CHAPTER 2

Simon Blackburn, *Ethics: A Very Short Introduction* (Oxford: Oxford University Press, 2003).

Bernard Williams, *Ethics and the Limits of Philosophy* (Cambridge, Mass.: Harvard University Press, 1985).

CHAPTER 3

Peter Singer, *Animal Liberation*, 2nd edn. (London: Harper Perennial, 2009).

Susan Armstrong (ed.), *The Animal Ethics Reader* (London: Routledge, 2008).

CHAPTER 4

Michael Sandel, *The Case Against Perfection: Ethics in the Age of Genetic Engineering* (New York: The Belknap Press, 2007).

John Harris, *Enhancing Evolution: The Ethical Case for Making Better People* (Princeton: Princeton University Press, 2007).

CHAPTER 5

Michael J. Pakaluk (ed.), *Other Selves: Philosophers on Friendship* (New York: Hackett, 1991).

Neera Kapur Badhwar, *Friendship: A Philosophical Reader* (New York: Cornell University Press, 1993).

CHAPTER 6

Kwame Anthony Appiah, *Cosmopolitanism: Ethics in a World of Strangers* (London: Penguin, 2007).

Joshua Cohen (ed.), *For Love of Country: Debating the Limits of Patriotism* (Boston: Beacon Press, 1996).

CHAPTER 7

Miranda Fricker, *Epistemic Injustice: Power and the Ethics of Knowing* (Oxford: Oxford University Press, 2007).

Karen Jones, 'The Politics of Credibility', in L. Antony and C. Witt (eds.), *A Mind of One's Own* (Boulder, Colo.: Westview Press, 2002; 2nd edn. *only*).

CHAPTER 8

Anne Phillips, *Multiculturalism Without Culture* (Princeton: Princeton University Press, 2007).

Joshua Cohen, Matthew Howard, and Martha C. Nussbaum (eds.), *Is Multiculturalism Bad for Women?* (Princeton: Princeton University Press, 1999).

CHAPTER 9

Will Kymlicka, *Multicultural Odysseys: Navigating the New International Politics of Diversity* (Oxford: Oxford University Press, 2007).

Anthony Simon Laden and David Owen (eds.), *Multiculturalsm and Political Theory* (Cambridge: Cambridge University Press, 2007).

CHAPTER 10

Wendy Brown, *Regulating Aversion: Tolerance in the Age of Identity and Empire* (Princeton: Princeton University Press, 2008).

John Locke, *A Letter Concerning Toleration* (1689).

CHAPTER 11

Tim Crane, *The Mechanical Mind*, 2nd edn. (London: Routledge, 2003).

John Searle, *Minds, Brains and Science: The 1984 Reith Lectures* (Harmondsworth: Penguin, 1984).

CHAPTER 12

David Papineau (ed.), *The Philosophy of Science* (Oxford: Oxford University Press, 1996).

T. S. Kuhn, *The Structure of Scientific Revolutions*, 3rd edn. (Chicago: University of Chicago Press, 1996).

CHAPTER 13

Barry Stroud, *The Significance of Philosophical Scepticism* (Oxford: Oxford University Press, 1984).

George Berkeley, *Treatise Concerning the Principles of Human Knowledge* (1710).

CHAPTER 14

D. H. Mellor, *Real Time II* (London: Routledge, 1998).

J. R. Lucas, *A Treatise on Time and Space* (London: Methuen, 1973).

CHAPTER 15

A. W. Moore, *The Infinite*, 2nd edn. (London: Routledge, 2001).

Eli Maor, *To Infinity and Beyond: A Cultural History of the Infinite* (Boston: Birkhäuser, 1986).

CHAPTER 16

Timothy Williamson, *Vagueness* (London: Routledge, 1994).

Rosanna Keefe and Peter Smith (eds.), *Vagueness: A Reader* (Cambridge, Mass.: MIT Press, 1996).

CHAPTER 17

Derek Matravers, *Art and the Emotions: A Defence of the Arousal Theory* (Oxford: Oxford University Press, 2001).

Nigel Warburton, *The Art Question* (London: Routledge, 2003).

CHAPTER 18

Alain de Botton, *The Architecture of Happiness* (London: Penguin, 2007).

Le Corbusier, *Towards a New Architecture* (New York: Dover, 2000).

CHAPTER 19

Barry C. Smith (ed.), *Questions of Taste* (Oxford: Oxford University Press, 2007).

David Hume, 'Of the Standard of Taste' (1757; in many editions of his essays).

CHAPTER 20

Alex Neill, 'Tragedy', in Berys Gaut and Dominic Lopes (eds.), *The Companion to Aesthetics* (London: Routledge, 2001).

Walter Kaufmann, *Tragedy and Philosophy* (Princeton: Princeton University Press, 1992).

CHAPTER 21

Don Cupitt, *Taking Leave of God* (London: SCM Press, 1980).

Robin Le Poidevin, *Arguing for Atheism* (London: Routledge, 1996).

CHAPTER 22

John Cottingham, *On the Meaning of Life* (London: Routledge, 2002).

Oswald Hanfling, *Life and Meaning* (New York: Wiley, 1987).

CHAPTER 23

Stephen Law, *Humanism: A Very Short Introduction* (Oxford: Oxford University Press, forthcoming).

M. McC. Adams and R. M. Adams (eds.), *The Problem of Evil* (Oxford: Oxford University Press, 1990).

CHAPTER 24

Keith Ward, *Concepts of God*, 2nd edn. (London: Oneworld, 1998).

Sue Hamilton, *Indian Philosophy: A Very Short Introduction* (Oxford: Oxford University Press, 2001).

CHAPTER 25

A. C. Grayling, *Ideas That Matter* (London: Weidenfeld, 2009).

Sam Harris, *Letter to a Christian Nation* (New York: Bantam, 2007).